The SPIRIT of a GODDESS

How To Reconnect to Your Wisdom, Power and Divine Femininity Within

CHE THE GODDESS

Copyright © 2020 The King's Daughter, LLC.
The Spirit of a Goddess - Second Edition, 2022
www.TkdCollective.com

All Rights Reserved. No part of this publication may be reproduced, stored in a retrieval system, or transmitted in any form or by any means (including electronic, mechanical, photocopying, recording, or otherwise) without prior written permission from the author.

While the author and publisher have used their best efforts in preparing this book, they make no representation or warranties with respect to the accuracy or completeness of the contents of this book. The author and publisher assume no responsibility for the results or outcomes resulting from the use of the information presented herein.

This book is intended for educational and informational purposes. It cannot be used as a substitute for professional advice. The ideas, information and guidelines may not be suitable for your personal situation. You should always consult a licensed physician wherever appropriate.

For information on special sales, bulk discounts and corporate purchases please contact support@tkdCollective.com

ISBN: 978-1-7359679-3-6

Special thanks to the amazing team that made my book cover photo possible:
Cover Photographer: @IslandBoiPhotography
Makeup: @KingKamate
Crown: @ReignGlobal

Book Cover Design & Interior by HMDpublishing
Book Editing by Nicole Draiss & Cathy McMahon

Join my free 21day Self-Love challenge at
WWW.THESPIRITOFAGODDESS.COM
*for daily guided meditation, sound
healing, resources, tips and more.*

BOOK DEDICATION

This book is dedicated to the beautiful, amazingly talented Goddess and Emmy award winning artist Hadiiya Barbel. Thank you for your visionary leadership, exceptional contribution to the Goddess movement and for awakening the Goddess within me.

BOOK REVIEWS

Epic, transformational, motivational guide for Goddesses from all walks of life. A must read...
—LAUREN VON DER POOL
Celebrity Chef & Best-selling author

This is an inspirational book that speaks to the heart, mind and soul of the reader. The author is open and transparent. I envision this book used for one's self-discovery and reflection...leading to a great impact on humanity.
—OCTAVIA SHAW
DC Public School Teacher

The content shared resonates in our current world allowing the reader to achieve spiritual nourishment and self-acceptance.
—RASHIDA JONES
CyberSecurity Analyst

This book speaks to true elevation and rising above our perceptions of success and greatness.
—KAREEMAH WOODARD
Well Fit Pro Personal Trainer

I salute, thank and honor the below Goddesses that have paved the way and upon whose shoulders I stand to bear this fruit.

QUEEN AFUA
The Queen Mother Goddess who teaches us to Heal Thyself

HADIIYA BARBEL
The Goddess of Feminine Liberation & Empowerment who teaches us to stand in our truth

SOLE AJAH SHAH
The Goddess of Love who teaches us to walk in love

LAUREN VON DER POOL
The Goddess of the Greens who teaches us to eat life to become life

CONTENTS

Chapter 1. *The Divine Feminine* 3

Chapter 2. *Intuition* 17

Chapter 3. *Purpose* 27

Chapter 4. *Love* 36

Chapter 5. *Divine Manifestation* 45

Chapter 6. *Total Wellbeing* 52

Chapter 7. *Leadership* 62

Chapter 8. *Relationships* 64

Chapter 9. *Struggle Is Only a Season* 77

Chapter 10. *Anxiety and Depression* 85

Chapter 11. *Spirit* 90

Chapter 12. *Energy* 97

Chapter 13. *The Shadow* 108

Chapter 14. *Eternal Life* 115

Chapter 15. *The Goddess Manifest* 119

INTRODUCTION

When I turned 40 in 2019, I was inspired to write the initial version of this book because I was in the midst of a Spiritual awakening. My dear friend Debbie and then my sister-in-law Ngozi had just passed away from breast cancer a year apart from each other. I was hit hard by both losses. I spent a lot of time in close proximity to both Debbie and Ngozi, praying with and counseling both leading up to their transition.

Shortly after my sister-in-law passed, I experienced a series of what I considered at that time to be personal tragedies, including a miscarriage and chronic illness. This threw me into a deep depression. I had to dig myself out of that hole inch by inch. It was a slow and painful process. I found out the hard way that it was much easier to counsel someone else than it was to take my own advice.

I embarked upon a personal quest to find a way to adjust to my new reality. In my search, I gained a new understanding of myself, my grief and a way out. From my breakdown came my biggest breakthroughs. Initially, I felt the need to document my breakthroughs as a life guide for my sons because they were profound experiences for me, which resulted in much peace of mind and the ability to identify and overcome many things that were invisibly holding me back.

After writing a few chapters, it hit me that my fellow Goddesses would benefit greatly from what I had to share. Women more often go out of their way in search of life solutions and then bring them back to their homes to share with their families. So, it all made sense to write this book as a Goddess book.

Everything you need shows up at exactly the time that you need it. There are no mistakes. Your reading of this book is, therefore, no random coincidence. It is in Divine Order because whatever you are seeking is also seeking you.

I am confident that whatever you are searching for, you will find (even if it is just a piece of it) within the pages of this book to help you along your life journey. So, I bow and honor the Divine in you.

1

The Divine Feminine

"When we embody our Divine Feminine Essence, this is the greatest gift we can give of ourselves to the world."

What I mean when I refer to a woman as a Divine Feminine Goddess? Divine is anything that is inspired by Source or an emanation from Source. Because we are Divine, we are, therefore, sacred.

In the past few years, there has been a rise of the Divine Feminine—a calling for all women around the world to rise up and embody our Divine Feminine Essence. This is the natural state most women are born into. Examples of our natural Divine Feminine qualities are compassion, creativity, intuition, empathy, and receptivity. We exhibit these qualities from simply BE-ing.

These qualities require us not to force anything to happen. Instead, we sit in a state of allowance and grace, trusting in our instinctive, natural divine power as feminine beings that all that is for us will come to us effortlessly and without struggle. We gracefully surrender to the ebbs and flows of life, knowing that all is always working out in our favor.

We sometimes shift out of this natural state as a survival instinct. This occurs frequently with women who have been through some trauma and take on a tough, almost emotionless exterior as a survival mechanism. It also often shows up when we take on leadership positions or are thrust into the role of a single mom, which require us to be assertive, somewhat forceful, decisive, and linear thinkers in order to be successful in these roles.

It is okay to sometimes shift out of our Feminine Essence because of the need to find a balance between our Masculine and Feminine aspects. The point is not to remain stuck there but to remember to drop back out of our heads into the softness of our hearts, whenever possible, to rest back into the true essence of our being.

When we embody our Divine Feminine Essence, we apply creative, intuitive, heartfelt thinking that allows for multiple points of consideration. This allows for diversity of thought and balance.

A woman fully embodying her natural Divine Feminine Essence is the greatest gift she can give of herself to the world. It is the settling into our authentic selves, embracing who we truly are, and being fully at ease with ourselves. It is not trying to blend into a male-dominated society but leading from your feminine seat of power with love and authenticity. Naturally, you become a force to be reckoned with, just like the waves of the ocean—soft and yielding, yet powerful and effective.

Our Divine Feminine qualities are sorely missing in our leadership today. Most men do not naturally possess these traits and most times have to step out of their Masculine Essence to embody these feminine qualities.

This is not to say that all masculine leadership traits are bad for our society, not at all. The *authentic, sacred Masculine* traits utilize courage and honor to guide the human race forward, which has resulted in boundless exploration and many innovative breakthroughs. However, there also exists the *inauthentic, non-sacred Masculine* traits of arrogance, greed, selfishness and heartlessness that have resulted in human rights abuse, materialism, war and death.

These inauthentic masculine traits are driven by people's deepest insecurities and fear and have caused a lot of disharmony in our world today. Leaders of various nations have put into use this inauthentic, self-centered leadership style, putting their interests ahead of those of their people.

This has thrown our world into chaos. Diplomacy has been set aside for the use of force, violence and manipulation. Because of this, there has been a disintegration of the moral fabric of our society, which has led to incessant bickering, dissent, divisiveness and hate. This disintegration has led to a sicker nation due to the increased amount of stress and tension placed on all involved.

A balance is needed between the authentic, sacred Masculine energies and the sacred Divine Feminine energies for there to be an equilibrium and harmony in our world today. An emergence of Divine Feminine leadership is needed to create a balance in an overly male-dominated world.

The emergence of COVID-19 in 2020 has forced the world to take a pause and re-evaluate how we, as individuals, have contributed to the collapse of the well- being of our people and planet. We have been called to create new ways of being in order to heal and uplift ourselves. The old ways are obviously not working for our planet. We, as women, have been called to rise up all over the world to take our rightful seat of power and be revered as sacred for the world to come back into harmony.

Prior to the COVID-19 pandemic, there was a slow but steady shift in the rise of the Divine Feminine. Women all over the world began to reawaken to their intrinsic inner power and Sovereignty. When COVID-19 hit, it threw the world into darkness. Self-care has become no longer an option, but a necessity, in order to survive the global cleansing. This has forced us to turn to nature for peace of mind and holistic remedies.

The source of your power as a Goddess is Self-Love. When you return home to Self by nurturing your Mind, Body and Spirit, you rise up. You experience a more present, joyful and serene Self—one radiating with an overflowing aura of abundance, contentment and peace.

The purpose of this book is to delve into multiple Spiritual principles, practices and teachings that will re-awaken you to the inner power that lies within you so that you can fully embody the *Spirit of the Goddess* every single waking day, no matter what is going on in the world around you.

THE RE-DEFINITION OF A GODDESS

When the word Goddess is mentioned, what comes to mind? Do you think of the archetypes of the Goddesses that you have been taught in the past like the African Goddesses Osun, Yemaya and Oya; Hindu Goddesses like Saraswati, Lakshmi and Parvati; or maybe even Greek Goddesses like Aphrodite, Athena and Artemis? This is one valid school of thought.

However, I'm going to redefine what it means to be a Goddess. To fully embody your Goddess-self, what if you didn't have to channel any particular Goddess archetype? What if instead, you could simply channel the highest version of yourself? This is because you are, in fact, the Goddess. The Goddess, my love is within you!

Allow me to re-introduce you to a different perspective of the Goddess as a way of BE-ing. When any woman of any race or background shows up as the highest version of herself, radiating light instead of darkness, she is showing up as the Goddess within her.

Being a Goddess isn't an isolated, moment-by-moment event that you turn on and off like a light switch— being Goddess-like in public but being *nasty and toxic* when dealing with everyday people. Most of us cave in when life throws us a curveball, and we fall off our seat of power. We succumb when things are not working out for us as they should. We succumb to failed relationships. We succumb to job loss. We succumb to people treating us badly. We succumb to and reflect back what is in front of us. This causes us to fall back into toxic cycles and patterns of behavior that we thought we had outgrown.

It is in challenging and difficult times that there is a greater need for you to show up as the Goddess that you are. That is when you are most desperately needed to inspire others to level up.

A Goddess brings a sense of calm and peace to any situation she walks into. She infuses the room with love—the highest vibration possible. She walks with integrity, speaks words of truth and healing, and showers others with blessings continuously, even through her own trials and tribulations.

In order to remain on your Sovereign seat of power, you must tune into yourself on the inside. You must adopt daily spiritual practices that will help you to anchor into a state of inner peace and equanimity regardless of what shows up in your life. When you have a solid foundation, you are not thrown off by toxic circumstances or toxic people that pop up unexpectedly in your life. No matter what shows up or how it shows up, you remain firmly rooted and grounded from a place of infinite peace and serenity.

A way to develop a place of deep, inner peace is by adopting a daily spiritual practice. This is so important but highly underestimated and, therefore, mostly overlooked. You should follow your spiritual practice on a daily basis. You can come up with your own, or you can repurpose my guided meditations offered on www.thespiritofagoddess.com to help you ground yourself back to your divinity.

A spiritual practice is basically a spiritual routine or ritual you do at the same time, every day. For example, at 5 a.m. each day, you pray/meditate for 30 minutes, next you immerse yourself in a spiritual bath for 20 minutes while listening to affirmations, then drink an herbal tea for 5 minutes, play spiritual music for 10 minutes, dance for 10 minutes, and lastly journal for 10 minutes. This is your daily spiritual practice each and every day—starting at 5 a.m. every single morning. Once you complete your spiritual practice, then you can begin your day with more clarity, calmness, focus and peace of mind.

When there is turmoil within her Spirit, she knows how to quickly return back to her center and get back in alignment with her higher Self. She forgives easily, but she never forgets because she loves herself and, therefore, protects her heart and energy always. She doesn't let herself be taken advantage of, abused or disrespected. She holds herself in high regard and knows her worth; therefore, she knows when to walk away.

She is magnetic. She shows up as the physical manifestation of the beauty that is within her, radiating love and light. She is *beauty* fully embodied. She is powerful beyond measure and a force to be reckoned with.

The effects of engaging with a Goddess

When you engage with a Goddess, you experience:

- Peace
- Love
- Gratitude
- Empowerment
- Inspiration
- Authenticity
- Integrity
- Hope
- Kindness
- Joy
- Beauty
- Strength

This will, then, inspire you to soften into your own Divine Feminine Essence and radiate your own inner light.

MY LIFE AS AN EMPATH

I am originally of West African descent; however, I was born in Los Angeles, California, in the late seventies. As a little girl, I was often told I was way too sensitive. Therefore, I viewed my hypersensitivity as something that needed to be either suppressed or ignored.

I noticed that I was frequently overwhelmed when people engaged in loud, incessant chatter around me for an extended period of time. I had this feeling of being overloaded, and it was challenging for me to actively engage in or process this over-stimulation. I would have to take some quiet time by myself, in silence and away from everyone, in order to recharge and return to feeling like myself again.

As I grew older, I learned that for every heavy social interaction, I needed some personal quiet time to recharge my energy. It was challenging for me to keep up with sustained, over-zealous interactions, as I found myself leaving early, arriving late or simply not wanting to go to large social events (especially where I didn't know a lot of the people personally) because it was way too much stimulation and overload for me.

In my late thirties, while working at an American corporation, I opted to take the Myers-Briggs Personality assessment as part of our team-building activity and discovered that I was an INTJ (Introvert-Judging). No surprise there that I was categorized as an introvert. By doing some more research into personality types during my personal time, I discovered that I am also an Empath.

What is an Empath, you may ask? Well, an Empath is a person with extraordinary perceptual abilities who unconsciously senses things in the unseen and seen realms. Empaths

naturally pick up on the energy of their surroundings and have a natural ability to tune into the feelings of others. Empaths make great healers, therapists, yoga instructors, psychics and mediums. Empaths are naturally very loving, highly compassionate beings.

Being an Empath is not something that is learned; either you are born an Empath, or you are not. An Empath is naturally able to pick up on other people's energy, sometimes get premonitions of certain events before they occur and receive incredible insight into their reality through visions, dreams and the like.

When I discovered I was an Empath, it brought a lot of clarity and meaning to what I had been experiencing my entire life. It put a name to the feeling I commonly get—like I am bearing the weight of the world on my shoulders.

It also empowered me to own ALL of me— my quirkiness, eccentricities, discomfort, pain—all of it. Granted, I was different. However, I realized it was not something to be ashamed of or hide from, wishing it would go away. It was something to embrace and seek empowerment from. What I previously viewed as a personality glitch, I now understand it to be a gift. This came after 38 years of me feeling like a misfit and sometimes wishing I could crawl out of my own skin because of the discomfort I often felt. From this newly found perspective, I was able to have a greater appreciation and understanding of who I am, and I finally began to fall in love with myself.

Everyone is born with intuition, which is your natural connection to a deep well of infinite, divine, cosmic, collective intelligence. Being an Empath builds upon this natural intuition. However, you don't have to be an Empath to be intuitive. You can work with what you have and be able to do quite a lot with it.

My Empathic traits help me connect better with others on a more deeper level. It enables me to have a genuine compassion and love for people. These traits allow me to open myself up and surrender to the path destined for me. Later on in this book, I will provide you with my unique methodology to help you identify your unique purpose on this Earth.

THE SELF

Before you learn about any Spiritual concepts, you have to start with the knowledge of Self. This is because you must master your Self before you can master anything else in life. The journey begins from within. When you fully understand who you are and what you are made of, then everything else will fall into place.

Diagram 1: *Inner Self vs. Outer Self*

Let's start with the Self. You are made up of an *Inner Self* and *Outer Self*.

Your *Inner Self* is made up of your Soul and Spirit.

Your *Soul* is your Consciousness. This is your unique identity or personality. Your Soul is basically *who you are* as a unique, individual being.

Your Consciousness is that inner voice in your head that talks to you non-stop all day long. It is essentially *you* talking to *you*, chattering non-stop—saying things about people and things around you, what you need to do next, or whether you like something or not. It's your awareness of your being in the here and now.

Your *Spirit* is the part of your Inner Self that is in constant communication with infinite intelligence. Your Spirit is a vessel within your Inner Self that can be occupied by various forms of energy. Your Spirit takes on whatever form of energy it is consistently exposed to—be it empowering or non-empowering.

Your Spirit is similar to a balloon that can be filled up with two different types of gases—one that can *lift you up,* like helium, or one that can *bring you down,* like carbon monoxide. It can also be *empty* and *deflated*. However, it does not stay *empty and deflated* for long because the Universe abhors a vacuum. Any space unoccupied in the Universe always eventually gets filled with something; hence, some energy will naturally seek to take the place of this vacuum within your Spirit.

This is why you have to daily fill your Spirit with positive thoughts, words, affirmations and prayers, else your environment will choose it for you—and most of the time it will fill you up with things that are of lower vibration. This is because this is the natural default programming of the world we live in—one of cynicism, self-doubt and pessimism.

The *Outer Self* is made up of our physical Body, through which we experience life. It is the means through which we have our physical interactions with the world around us. We interact with our world through our five senses of taste, touch, smell, sight and hearing.

When you die, your Inner Self (Soul and Spirit in unison) leaves your physical Body (or Outer Self) and transitions into the Spiritual realm, continuing on in its infinite existence. Your Inner Self's occupation within your physical Body is what gives your physical Body its life, vitality and unique personality.

We are Spiritual beings temporarily existing in our physical bodies on this earth for a limited amount of time. Therefore, we don't have a lot of time to waste. We have a dual (*Earthly* and *Spiritual*) purpose to fulfill on this earth—to uplift the Collective consciousness of our planet. If you do not fulfill your Spiritual purpose on this earth, something is left undone and missing in the Spiritual realm that would have contributed to the fullness of a divine plan set in motion by the Creator. Therefore, every Soul's purpose matters. When your purpose is not fulfilled, there is a void in the divine scheme of things.

Someone's life can be extended by your thoughts, words or actions; likewise, someone's life can be cut short by your thoughts, words or actions. This is because your thoughts are things, and they eventually manifest in the world as action taken. The entire planet can be wiped out by your singular action (think of the lab technician in Wuhan, China). On the other hand, think of Martin Luther King, Jr., whose ideas, words, and actions created a global paradigm shift. Your Soul's wisdom is infinite.

Your Soul existed before you were born. When you are physically born into this world, you are born into a state of amnesia as to who you truly are. As we progress in life, we slowly come into a state of remembrance of who we truly are—our Soul's true identity. This lets us know why we are here and what our Soul has come to accomplish on this earth. When we connect to Source energy, we are able to tap into an infinite pool of cosmic intelligence and Divine power to manifest things that we never thought were possible.

2

Intuition

"The intuitive mind is a sacred gift and the rational mind is a faithful servant."

—A<small>LBERT</small> E<small>INSTEIN</small>

Do you know that uneasy feeling you get around someone you just met that you can't quite put your finger on, but you just know that something isn't right? It can also manifest as that instinctive dislike for someone you barely even know because their energy just doesn't feel right. This is your intuition (or intuit side) picking up on the unseen.

Definition of *intuition*

1 a : the power or faculty of attaining to direct knowledge or cognition without evident rational thought and inference

Merriam Webster

Merriam-Webster defines intuition as the above. Similarly, *Wikipedia* defines intuition as the ability to understand something immediately without the need for conscious reasoning. Therefore, intuition happens on a subconscious level. In science, intuition is described as your connection to an infinite Collective consciousness through your subconsciousness. Great Leaders like Oprah Winfrey ascribe their success to having followed their intuition to make smart decisions, even in difficult circumstances.

Intuition tends to arise *without* conscious awareness of the underlying facts or information. Psychologists define it as nonconscious thinking that is not based on evidence of rational thought or reasoning. It is sometimes described in simple terms as your *gut feeling* or a *hunch*.

Intuition is described by many experts as the highest form of human intelligence. A rational thought may provide you with a logical reason as to why you need to do something; however, it's that gnawing feeling that brings into your awareness the possibility that you're most likely making a bad decision. Your intuition usually ends up being right.

Albert Einstein has been widely quoted as saying, "the intuitive mind is a sacred gift and the rational mind is a faithful servant." However, we have created a society that honors the servant and ignores the gift. Your intuition is a gift that is there to help guide you away from danger but also advance you towards moments of opportunity.

Your intuition is your Superpower. It is your Divine compass guiding you through life. It is your access to Divine intelligence that is gifted to you by the Creator.

Everything that happens to you is in Divine order. Nothing happens by accident or out of order. This includes your so-called "mistakes." They are all perfectly and divinely timed for your current version of Self to receive the lesson it needs, in order to meet your next moment of opportunity with preparedness.

You are surrounded by infinite possibilities—and either way, the path you end up choosing is one of many *right* possibilities that leads you down a path towards gaining the wisdom you need for the next phase of your journey.

Even if you choose a *"wrong"* path, it would still be the *right* path for you. This is because you are signaling to the Universe that you are not ready for the *right* path and need the rehashing or reinforcement of a prior life lesson. This is why sometimes, you may notice the same toxic, negative circumstances keep repeating itself in your life, only with different people involved, but it's the same old script. This continues on repeat until you fully master that specific life lesson. When the lesson is mastered, a new *right* path will become more attractive to you because it is now more in alignment with your preparedness for the next phase of your journey.

On September 11, 2001, Seth McFarlane, creator of the series *Family Guy*, was scheduled to be aboard American Airlines Flight 11, which was the first to hit the World Trade Center. He had a hangover the morning of his flight and ended up missing it by just ten minutes. His "mistake" ended up being his saving grace, perfectly and divinely timed, which ended up saving him from a fatal plane crash.

Your intuition is God-given. You are born with it. You are connected to your intuition through your *third eye*. Some refer to it as your *sixth sense* and it is located in your *third eye chakra* or *ajna*. Some Spiritual traditions suggest the third eye serves as a metaphysical connection between the physical and Spiritual worlds. It is believed to be your Divine connection to the unseen realm. Your Spiritual downloads are believed to happen through your third eye. Meditation or any calming, grounding activity is believed to strengthen your third eye, which in turn strengthens your intuition.

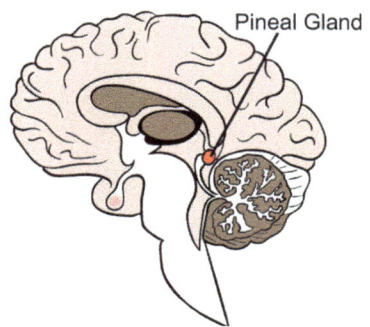

Diagram 2: *Pineal gland*

INTUITION VS. FEAR

Intuition can manifest either as a positive feeling or as a negative premonition. This is why people sometimes have a hard time telling whether what we are feeling is linked to a *subconscious underlying fear* from past experiences, or if it is indeed their *intuition* working to keep them away from danger. *Fear* and *intuition* can come up as very strong feelings, and therefore, can get confused very easily. It is therefore important to be able to distinguish between the two.

For example, there is no evidence for you to feel uncomfortable about a particular person, but you do because there is an energetic exchange where you have this knowing that this person's aura just doesn't feel right.

Author and Coach Marie Forleo describes *fear* as a contractive feeling, whereas *intuition* is an expansive feeling. With fear, you feel a sense of dread, and your Body pulls in. However, with intuition, you experience a feeling where your Body opens up in an expansive way.

The *fear* you feel, in contrast to *intuition*, is caused by your negative past experiences, environment, upbringing, or social conditioning towards a person, group of people or situation. Your intuition, in contrast to fear is you being informed by an infinite intelligence that is far greater and more expansive than any thought any one person has.

Spiritual teacher and Guru Deepak Chopra describes *intuition* as an epiphany or insight that happens in the spontaneity of the stillness of the mind, helping you to make evolutionary choices—one for your highest good. He, however, distinguishes *fear* as simply your anxiety at play.

Intuition guides you into taking actions toward your highest good. However, fear manipulates you into taking actions from a place of lack, which ends up not being aligned for your higher good.

HOW TO DEEPEN YOUR INTUITION

Everyone has some level of intuition. However, Empaths usually have a stronger intuition than others. All is not lost if your intuition is not as strong as you would like it to be. There are ways you can work to strengthen it so it can work better for you.

Here are four ways to deepen your intuition:

1. **Meditate regularly:** Meditation is defined as the conscious attempt to retrain your brain to get out of analytical, ruminating thoughts and be fully present in the now. When we meditate, we quieten our minds of the internal chatter and outside noise, which allows us to hear the soft whispers of infinite intelligence and divine guidance. With practice, it becomes easier to pick up on divine guidance, and thus, making your intuit abilities more quickly accessible to you.

2. **Take regular quiet walks:** Taking daily quiet walks is a way to quieten the mind and allow new intuitive thoughts to flow in.

3. **Spend time alone in silence:** Spending time alone in silence is a great way to calm the mind, relax the Body and allow you to tap into the infinite pool of Source consciousness and intelligence.

4. **Perform Grounding activity:** Grounding is a means of releasing stored up negative ions that have accumulated within the Body that can lead to stress and anxiety. This is done by spending time in nature or simply walking bare feet on the earth.

Meditation Activity
- Go into a quiet room by yourself, preferably.

- Turn down the lights. Light a scented candle with essential oils like lavender, eucalyptus oil, sandalwood or sage.

- You can opt to smudge with Palo Santo (Holy wood) to attract good energy into your space or sage to remove negative energy from your space. Leave your windows open while smudging with sage to let out the negative energy.

- Once you've cleansed your space, put on your favorite slow, soft, soothing music.

- Get into a calm state of Mind and Body.

- Quiet your Mind by getting rid of any distracting noise or movements around you.

- Relax your Body by sitting in a cross-legged position on your yoga mat, loosening up your shoulders, relaxing your jawline and anywhere there is tension.

- Open up your arms and lay them softly on your knees in an upwards position.

- Slowly take a deep breath in through your nostrils and hold it for three seconds, then release it out through your mouth. Repeat five times.

- Continue to breathe slowly, but only through your nostrils.

- Do not use this time to plan out your day or think analytically about anything.

- ⊙ Keep your Mind empty of any remnant thoughts and focus solely on your breathing. This means allowing your Mind to fully savor every molecule of air coming in and out of your nostrils.

If your Mind drifts away to worrying about things you have to get done for the week or problems you need to solve, it's okay and totally normal for you to experience this. Again, bring your attention back solely on your breathing. Meditation is simply retraining your attention. Like anything else, with more practice, it becomes easier to do.

In summary, for at least 60 minutes each day, meditate until you clear your Mind of any lingering thoughts. If your Mind starts to wander, bring it back to the present moment and focus solely on the observance of your breathing.

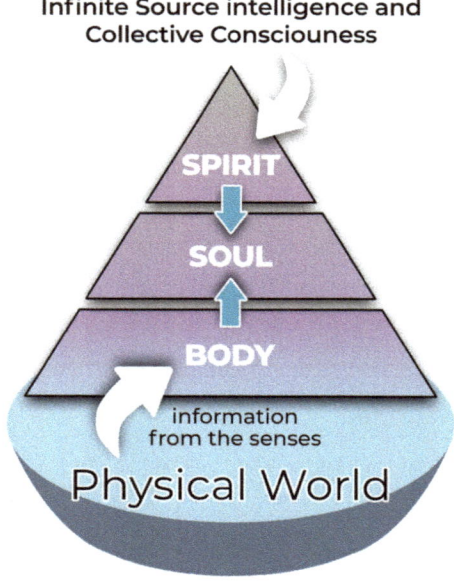

Diagram 3: *Spirit, Soul, Body interaction*

Source intelligence is made available to us in our moments of silence and stillness. If you are constantly on the go, it is hard to access this information. Meditation helps to quieten the Mind, which deepens your intuitive ability to pick up on the infinite wisdom available to you, to help guide you along your life's journey.

INSPIRATION

> *"The highest human act is to inspire."*
> —**Nipsey Hussle**

You can inspire others when you show unconditional love, forgiveness, patience, kindness, humility, resilience, courage or generosity to another. If you can inspire just one person, it can spark a flame that can light up the entire world. *To inspire* or *be inspired* is what creates change around the world.

Inspiration can cause millions of people to experience a paradigm shift. Inspiration can serve to elevate consciousness. You can inspire others to do things they ordinarily would never have been inclined to do—such as being less judgmental, less homophobic or simply just being more open to a different point of view.

Inspiration is obtained from the things and people around us—our *environment*. It can come from nature, the communities we grew up in, our families, friends, the people we meet, what we see on TV, our leaders, and so on. Inspiration is normally drawn from things that are around us that are earth-based.

"Inspiration is like fine threads tugging at your Soul, reminding you of who you truly are, in order to bring you back into alignment with your authentic Self."

—Che the Goddess

Where inspiration goes, creativity flows. When you are inspired, you are in your highest creative flow. Inspiration causes feelings of joy within you when you follow its call. This is because when you are obedient to your inspiration, you become in alignment with your authentic Self. This is where the magic happens.

Great empires were brought into existence, cities erected, laws passed, and inventions made from a single spark of inspiration. Reverend Martin Luther King Jr., Mahatma Gandhi and President Barack Obama are all figures of great inspiration who ended up impacting the entire world, starting with a small spark of inspiration. One person really can impact global change, and that person can be you.

3

Purpose

"It doesn't interest me what you do for a living. I want to know what you ache for and if you dare to dream of meeting your heart's longing"

—Oriah Mountain Dreamer
from "The Invitation"

You may ask questions such as, "How do I find my purpose?", "Why am I here?", "What am I born to do?" or "What will bring my greatest joy and fulfillment?" These are questions that begin to occupy your mind as you journey through life and try to find your place in this worldly maze. When we step out into the world, we are consistently searching to find out who we truly are, what we are here for, and how we fit into this big puzzle called life.

One of the most impactful lessons my father taught me is that nothing in life happens by accident. Every person we meet and every event we encounter is part of an intricate, carefully orchestrated, highly organized, Divine plan. It looks disorganized at first, but looking back at his eighty-plus years of life, he sees how everything perfectly and divinely lined up to keep him alive, well and progressing along the path of an incredible life.

When he needed something, someone showed up out of nowhere and provided it to him. When he was lonely, someone showed up and comforted him. When he was broke, unable to pay for college and thought of giving up, someone showed up and paid for his tuition. When he had no family and no place to lay his head when he first arrived in the United States from Africa, a family took him under their wing and nurtured him. When my father hit his octogenarian milestone birthday in 2017, he looked back in amazement at the unique people and opportunities that presented themselves in his life. It was clear to him that all of life, as chaotic as it might seem and feel, actually is in Divine order and part of a larger, intelligently organized plan. Everything is in Divine order!

The moral of the story is what you *need* (when you are in alignment with your Divine path) will always show up *when* you need it. When you are out of alignment with your Divine path, what you need will show up as a *redirection* to your Divine path.

WHAT IS MY PURPOSE?

Your *Earthly purpose* serves to elevate the Collective Consciousness of the planet. When operating in your Earthly purpose, your job, essentially, is to leave the earth better than you met it.

In contrast, your *Spiritual purpose* is the Soul agreement you made before you were conceived in your mother's womb. When achieved, it contributes to the fullness of a bigger, Divine plan.

Therefore, every Soul matters. When your purpose is not fulfilled, something becomes permanently missing in the divine scheme of things. This is why fulfilling your Spiritual purpose is so important.

Earthly Purpose

Your Earthly purpose consists of your *Pleasure Purpose* and *Pain Purpose*.

Pleasure Purpose

Your *Pleasure Purpose* includes the activities you engage in that make you come alive and sets your heart on fire. Your Soul dances for joy whenever you engage in these activities. You have dreamed all your life about doing these activities or being this person. These activities effortlessly bring you immense joy. They come naturally to you, and you are born gifted with these attributes. You do them without much effort, to the bewilderment and respect of others.

For example, my Pleasure Purpose is dance and art. These two things are something I've always been naturally gifted at. I'd be the last one boogying on the dance floor in my family living room after hours of dancing with my siblings. My mom used to call me "*twiggy*" because of my natural rhythm coupled with my slim build. I also love to draw and paint. Both dancing and art come effortlessly to me, and I'm great at both.

What's *your* Pleasure Purpose? What do you love to do that lights you up, and makes your Soul soar? Let's journal about it below.

ACTIVITY:

1. *When you let your Mind wander while thinking of a liberating activity, what comes to Mind? Write these specific activities down.*
2. *As a child, what did you envision yourself becoming, based on things you were naturally good at but never quite pursued for whatever reason?*

The activities you have just listed are linked to your *Pleasure Purpose*.

Pain Purpose

The second type of purpose is your *Pain Purpose*. These are linked to your greatest struggles in life, the things that kicked your butt and made you almost give up. However, the warrior Goddess in you emerged and either overcame the struggle or found a way to manage the situation really well such that you are able to live a well-balanced, productive, happy life in spite of your circumstances—one an observer would initially have viewed as a tragedy, chastisement or permanent handicap.

This type of struggle opens the doorway to allow you to elevate the planet's Collective Consciousness. This is why you were born. This purpose is harder to follow because you got your butt kicked and handed to you, and once you overcame your struggles or learned to manage them really well, you just wanted to keep it a secret for fear of being judged or revisiting the pain of it all. It is something you may have lamented over in private to your family members or closest friends. You think about it from time to time, but then you hide it from everyone else to give the illusion of a normal life in order to blend into your interpretation of society's accepted standards and expectations.

> *"Sometimes you need to feel the sting and pain of defeat to activate the real purpose that God has predestined for you."*
> —CHADWICK BOSEMAN

Beloved, know this. You cannot elevate the planet's consciousness by hiding out in your bedroom under the covers, on your sofa flipping channels or behind your computer. You are called to meet your challenges fully with resilience, courage and determination, and once overcome, return and take others by the hand with you and help them over the hurdle. By sharing your story, you help others who are going through the same challenges to work through their pain, knowing that there is light at the end of the tunnel. The strength it took for you to overcome your pain and struggle will inspire others you share your story with to persevere through similar circumstances.

ACTIVITY:

Write your top five Pleasure Purposes and top five Pain Purposes. Over the next 30-90 days, your goal is to pursue at least one of your top Pleasure Purposes. Whenever you want to pursue something, write down key tasks you need to take to make it a reality. For example,

I Want to Become a Professional Model:

1. *Hire a photographer and take a professional photoshoot. (Due: Month 1)*

2. *Email your portfolio to the top five local modeling agencies. (Due: First half of Month 2)*

3. *Follow up with an email or phone call to make an appointment. (Due: Second half of Month 2)*

4. *Book my first gig. (Due: Month 3)*

Then you should work on meeting the deadlines you established in Steps 1-4 above because, as you know, a goal without a deadline is nothing but a wish.

Your Pleasure and Pain Purpose (i.e., your Earthly purpose) lead to the elevation of global consciousness and the advancement of our planet. It is through this means that you fulfill your divine duty of leaving this planet better than you found it—whether it be through art, medicine, music, dance, scientific breakthroughs, retreats, poetry or therapy. Whatever it is, it's up to you to transform the status quo. If you leave the world the same way you met it with no impact whatsoever, you've wasted your existence on earth.

Spiritual Purpose

The second type of purpose is your *Spiritual purpose*. If you do not fulfill your Spiritual purpose on this earth, there is something that becomes missing in the Spiritual realm that would have contributed to the fullness of a bigger divine plan set in motion by the Creator. No one can accomplish your purpose except you.

Your *Earthly purpose* prepares you and leads you up to your *Spiritual purpose*. You discover your Earthly purpose through inspiration. Inspiration is initiated from what goes on around you—the people you surround yourself with, the programs you watch, the environment you grow up in, the friends you keep, the music you listen to, the family you are born into.

You, however, get to discover your Spiritual purpose through your life's challenges, allowing your *intuition* to be your guide. *Your i*ntuition allows you to gain wisdom from infinite Source intelligence. You ask a question and get an answer. You are always connected to an infinite supply of wisdom, knowledge and supreme intelligence. It is always there waiting for you to tap into.

Your Spirit gives you Divine guidance and insight to allow you to make decisions that are most beneficial to your Soul and aligned with your authentic Self. For example, my Earthly purpose is art and dance. I used my artistic side to create a jewelry collection, TkdCollective.com (The King's Daughter Goddess Collective), and a women's athleisurewear company, Gymbreeze.com. This is because I want to use my gifts to the fullest of my ability and take inspired action whenever possible towards achieving my goals, dreams and desires.

ACTIVITY:

If you would like to receive Divine guidance on something of importance to you, do the following:

1. *Sit still in a quiet room or space. Clear your Mind of any residual thoughts or worry. Assure yourself that all is well and that you are safe and protected.*

2. *Allow yourself to come into a deeply relaxing, calm state by sitting in silence.*

3. *Ask the questions you want answered and pause.*

4. *Breathe slowly and deeply.*

5. *Pause and let your Mind wander as it filters in the answers and messages from the Divine that come to Mind. You might get visuals, words or ideas.*

6. *Write them down and use them as your starting point.*

7. *Meditate on the Divine guidance and wisdom you just received so as to fully understand its meaning and interpretation for your life. If it is unclear, share with a trusted person who can help you interpret your vision. The answers will also fully unfold with time because you have asked the question and unlocked the Cause and Effects powers of the Universe.*

8. ***Use your interpretation of these answers as a guide to get to your next level of evolution.***

When you desire something and ask for guidance. The Universe is always on your side and working in your favor.

You will notice over the next few weeks that people will pop into your life to align you with what you have asked for. The right people and circumstances will show up effortlessly to provide you that which you seek. There are things I have desired, and time and time again, I have had people walk into my life and deliver on what I have asked for.

4

Love

*"Love is the highest vibrational frequency
and most powerful force that exists."*

As the great Whitney Elizabeth Houston belted out one of her most famous songs in the 80s, "The Greatest Love of All," her powerful voice reverberated through the airwaves of our homes, melted our hearts, and we nodded in agreement that Self-Love is, indeed, the greatest love of all. Self-Love *truly* is the greatest love of all.

As a Goddess, Self-Love is your Superpower. However, for you to become anchored unto a solid, unshakeable foundation, you must be rooted in something bigger than yourself. Just like a light bulb taps into a power source to light it up, you must also tap into Source energy—which is also your power Source. Call upon the Divine to take residence within you, and continuously renew yourself with this forever expanding and boundless love.

You are most likely familiar with the saying *"God is love." This is true. God or Goddess* (if you will) is truly the purest embodiment of love. It is in the context of this highest standard of unconditional love that we possess the capability of truly loving ourselves and others fully. This is because God/Goddess lives within us and in others; therefore, we are never separate but always interconnected.

Unconditional love is accepting another fully, always wanting what's best for them. When you love someone unconditionally, you root for them to win the same way you would root for yourself to win. When you love someone unconditionally, you tell them the truth, even when it feels uncomfortable.

Know that love already exists within you because God/Goddess lives within you. You do not need to find or chase love. You just have to remember who you are. Sometimes that love is lying dormant from the effects of trauma, neglect, abandonment or pain. If this is the case, it just needs to be re-awakened.

To attract a love partner to you, you have to become that which you seek. If you desire love, be a loving person. Show up as a walking, breathing embodiment of love. When you do so, you attract those who vibrationally resonate on that same high frequency of love to you. On the other hand, if you *chase* love (a man or a relationship), it becomes elusive to you. It's like an animal in the wild. When you chase an animal, it runs away. Chasing also has *lack* written all over it. You have to magnetize that which you seek by becoming what it is. Attract love by becoming loving, and then you will attract *who* and *what* you are.

If it is meant to be, it will be. You will not have to force, chase, convince, beg or manipulate anyone into a relationship with you. Let it flow. Do not be attached to an outcome. Let it be what it is. Let it come to you. You are attracting everything you need. Trust in its Divine timing.

HOW TO BE A MAGNETIC GODDESS

We are created as Divine Feminine beings. We have traits that come naturally to us, like our softness, sensuousness, receptivity and nurturing qualities. When we do not take good care of ourselves, we begin to feel depleted. Spiritual teacher Aja Solé Shah, the recording artist formerly known as *Sole*, has one of the best teachings on being a Magnetic Goddess. Her teachings are very profound and enlightening.

Solé likens oneself to a garden that you have to nourish and water each day. Whenever you neglect a garden, it begins to die. Its beauty and radiance begin to fade away. In the same way, when you neglect yourself, your radiance, vitality and magnetism begin to fade away. The way you care for your Temple Body is by pouring into yourself. You do so by practicing self-care activities.

Get to know yourself deeply. Appreciate and celebrate the very essence of your being. Create joy within yourself to the point where there is an overflow. When you do so, you create a deep well within yourself that you can always return to and resource from whenever you feel depleted.

Solé teaches us to get into the habit of cultivating our *inner garden* and filling our cup on a daily basis so as not to let your well run dry. Examples of Spiritual practices that refill your cup are prayer, taking daily

Spiritual baths, meditation and sacred movement. Try as much as possible to spend quality time on activities centering on just you, by you, and for you, and this will begin to refill your cup.

I know this can be challenging for a lot of women as a lot of us are juggling a lot; running households, raising kids, running businesses and taking care of aging parents, however it is very possible and can be done. You just need to block out time and be strict about not letting any distractions get in the way. You should treat it as you would your fixed work schedule and hold yourself and others accountable for honoring your "me" time.

Tend to your inner garden daily. Self-care starts with Self-Love. When you love yourself, you take good care of yourself. When you take good care of yourself, you become happy, grounded and peaceful. From daily practice, you can achieve an abundant overflow of Self-Love. From this overflowing fountain of Self-Love, you can now invite a mate or spouse to partake in your already present overflow of joy, inner peace and fulfillment. You do not need a man to make you happy. You make yourself happy; then you invite a man to share in your already present joy. A man who comes into the picture should essentially partake in the overflow that you've already cultivated for yourself.

You cannot give from a state of depletion or lack. If you do not fill your cup, you will begin to look for happiness outside of yourself and seek validation from others. This forces you to step down from the throne of your Divine Feminine Sovereignty to chase, force or get a man to want you. "You fall into toxic relationships where you are desperate and need someone other than yourself to make you feel whole, complete and fulfilled. Your fulfillment should come from within you. You need to cultivate that inner garden so that you are always able to return to yourself to sip from your cup of overflowing Self-Love, whenever you need to. No person or relationship can offer you a sense of wholeness and completeness. It comes from your inner work."

The goal is for you to become love—one of the highest frequencies of vibration possible. We should strive every day to be in love with every aspect of ourselves—flaws and all. In this form, we become magnetic beings "regardless of our outer appearance, as our outer Self is merely a reflection of the inner light within us."

When we are in love with ourselves and life, we magnetize what we want. This is a powerful place to be. We must also get to know ourselves deeply. Solé describes it as "exploring one's inner terrain to allow us to discover who we truly are and what it is that we want and desire, in order to help us build a strong foundation that we can return to at any time."

To build a strong foundation to keep you from toxic relationships, cultivate your own support through a trusted circle of female friends with whom you easily relate to. When you are around other women, share your joys and challenges and provide support for one another. This is part of building your *inner garden* to come home to. Being around other women will also help activate more of the femininity within you as you commune and share in a sacred circle.

Solé tells us, "Find other passions you enjoy. Go out and meet new people. Cultivate new friendships. Lean on your circle of trusted women for support in times of loneliness so that you don't run back to a toxic relationship in times of isolation. Create a happy life for yourself that keeps you fulfilled irrespective of whether you have a man in your life or not." Being happy and having your own life and interests is very attractive to anyone—especially to a potential spouse.

HOW TO EMBODY LOVE

Embodiment is the representation of a thought or feeling in the physical form. We embody love when we are the physical representation of love. When we walk as love, talk as love, feel as love, live as love and fully represent the essence of love, we become love. This starts with deeply knowing yourself and loving yourself unconditionally. When we fully accept ourselves as we are, and have compassion for our imperfections, knowing that it is simply an expression of the amazing beauty and uniqueness of our being, then are we able to truly and profoundly love ourselves. This abundant overflow of love emanates from deep within us and is reflected to those around us. We then become a walking embodiment of love, and it radiates powerfully from the very core of our being.

When we are at this highest vibration, our aura begins to grow and expand outwards. People can feel our positive energy even ffrom across the room. It is a very powerful and attractive force.

Highest frequencies: Love and gratitude

Love and gratitude are the two highest vibrational frequencies. Love and gratitude attract more love and gratitude. Your expressions of love generate feelings of gratitude from yourself or others. Expressions of gratitude from yourself or others cause more love to be present. As you can see, there is a symbiotic relationship between the two.

Gratitude and Abundance

Gratitude magnetizes abundance. This is because when you are grateful, the Universe conspires to give you more things to be grateful for. This is part of the Universal Law of Cause and Effect. Michael Beckwith, founder of the Agape Center and contributor to the best-selling book *The Secret*, likens this to a mother telling her child, "If you don't stop crying, I'll give you something to cry about." In the same way, the Universe energetically says to us, "If you don't stop being grateful, I'll give you something to be grateful for." I thought this was a perfect and humorous analogy.

Lowest frequencies: Fear and anger

Fear and anger are the lowest vibrational frequencies. Fear and anger attract more fear and anger.

You are at your best when you are joyful and vibrating high. Therefore, never let anyone pull you down with their negativity or insecurities. Instead, have them level up to meet you at your higher vibration. It is easy to give in to resignation and cynicism because this is the more common, socially accepted way of being. Instead, vibrate high with love, kindness and compassion.

Do you know studies have shown it takes five affirmative statements to counteract one statement of disempowerment or negativity? That is why listening to affirmations is so powerful because it retrains your subconscious mind into positive Self-belief.

Speak words of life over yourself and your family constantly (using the "I AM" Affirmations in Chapter 5 below). Remind yourself of how amazing you are each day. Remind others around you of their beauty, grace and power. Remind them of what's possible.

CALLING FOR LOVE

> *"No problem can be solved from the same level of consciousness that created it."*
> —ALBERT EINSTEIN

People are either vibrating on the vibration of love, or on a vibration other than love. This other vibration is "calling for love." Reverend Michael Beckwith, founder of the Agape Center and contributor to the book *The Secret*, teaches us that when you meet the "calling for love" vibration with a vibration of love, you can lift up that lower vibration to that of love. The problems we have at one level of consciousness don't exist at a higher level of awareness. This is based on the Albert Einstein theory above, which holds true. You simply cannot solve a problem from the same level of consciousness that created it. You have to elevate. Most times, when you elevate, the problem simply no longer exists.

An easy way of choosing a higher consciousness is to come at the problem from an opposite perspective. For example, you soothe a hostile environment of hate with a higher vibration of love. You conquer a lower vibration of fear with a higher vibration of gratitude.

Love is the universal language of the Universe.

A Spiritual person recognizes the oneness in all of creation, honors this oneness, and lives a life of reverence for all of creation. Spirituality is the culmination of the love and reverence of Self, others and Mother Earth. I've noticed that every major Spiritual practice or religion is based on love. This is because love is a Universal language. No matter where you come from, or what language you speak, love transcends all. It is understood by all. It needs no interpretation.

In the hardest of situations and the toughest of times, when your back is against the wall, and you have nowhere to turn, turn to Love. It will give you peace of Mind and comfort in the midst of chaos, uncertainty and despair. It has *always* worked for me.

LOVE MANTRAS:

- I am loved.
- I am loved beyond measure
- I give and receive love fully and abundantly.

5

Divine Manifestation

*If you have faith the size of a mustard
seed, you can move mountains.*

Why do you look so anxious and worried? Beloved, do you realize how much power is within you? You have immense power that has already been bestowed upon you. We have been created with unfathomable power that we seldom recognize nor tap into. We look up into the sky and cry out for help, pleading and begging, not realizing that all that we need is already within us.

THE POWER OF DECLARATION

Let's talk about our inherent power of declaration. As you declare what you want, you must believe that which you declare to be true in order to manifest your intentions into existence. This is what I call your Divine right of Manifestation.

When you pray, don't stay in a continuous cycle of begging and pleading. Ask for what you want. Then stop! Believe it is already yours. Feel gratitude as you visualize what you have asked for coming into existence.

Gratitude creates an imbalance in the Universe that manifests things you can actually be grateful for. The more gratitude you have, the more things will be provided to you to be grateful for. This is because the Universe works in a balancing and cyclical manner. The Universe has been tasked to serve us and provide for our needs and desires. The Universe is at your service, and once you say what it's going to be, it immediately goes into motion to bring it into physical existence.

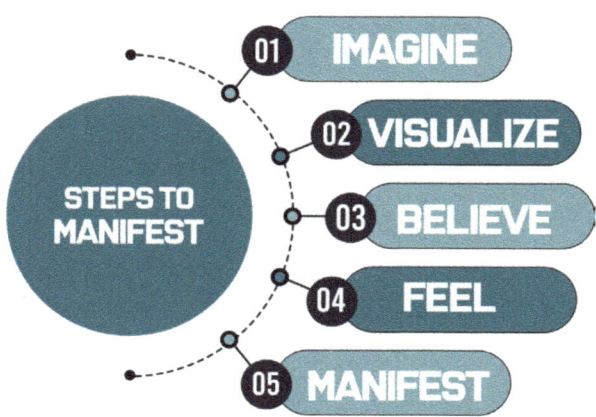

Diagram 15: *Steps to Manifest*

Life and Death lies at the power of the tongue

Our words are powerful. They have the power to create and the power to destroy; the power to heal and the power to hurt. Therefore, be very careful with what you say, as the Universe is called into action to manifest the words coming out of your mouth.

For example, when you wake up and you say, "I hate my job," the Universe goes into action to cause what you said to be true, creating more reasons why you should hate your job. So instead, find the little things that are working and give thanks for the small wins. Use that same energy to switch it around to attract better workmates or a better workplace by instead saying, "I am creating a work environment of joy, collaboration and appreciation." Then show up as that which you desire and watch the Universe go to work for you. A healthy workplace will be magnetized to you, if not in your current work environment, then in the form of a new work opportunity that comes knocking at your door shortly after.

There are two types of manifestation—*Direct manifestation* and *Aligned manifestation*. In Direct manifestation, we manifest from what we think we want based on what we see around us and what others have. However, in Aligned manifestation, our manifestation is fully aligned with our Soul's purpose. This can be likened to a seed planted in fertile soil, and you are simply asking for what is already within you to be birthed and come forth.

Where attention goes, energy flows.

When you focus on what's working, energy flows to magnify what is working, and then you have more things to be grateful for. Stand in gratitude of your small wins, and you will be provided more things to be grateful for.

Lastly, when you are manifesting, ask for what you want, *not* what you don't want. Don't make the mistake of inadvertently manifesting that which you *do not* desire. When you repeatedly ask for something *not* to happen, the Universe does not understand or process the word "*not*" or any negations in your request. It delivers on the request without the negation, and you end up attracting what you asked *not* to happen into your world.

So, instead of asking for what you *don't* want, ask for what you *do* want. I've made the mistake of manifesting things I did not want into my life by making this mistake, until I learned what the problem was. Make it clear by stating *what you want*. Read that again. It's a fine line, but it's very vital in manifestation. For example, instead of saying "I don't want to be sick" say "I am well" or "I fully embrace and appreciate the wellbeing of my body".

When we ask for *what we don't want not to occur*, we are, in essence, sending out feelings of fear and lack, which are of a low vibration. We attract to us things that are a vibrational match to what we are. The Universe automatically, by law, begins to pull in and attract to you the things that you vibrationally resonate with. These things become the thoughts of low frequency of the things you say you don't want. So, remember, ask for what you want, not what you don't want.

I AM THAT I AM

The words "I AM" are two of the most powerful words of creation, as the words you insert after them shape your reality. When you speak "I AM" Self-affirmations, you cause these positive qualities to become true for you. For example, here are some of my favorite powerful I AM affirmations that can help to reshape your reality right at this very moment:

- I AM…whole, perfect and complete
- I AM…beautiful
- I AM… strong
- I AM… confident
- I AM… fearfully and wonderfully made
- I AM… blessed with favor
- I AM… enough
- I AM… worthy
- I AM... patient
- I AM… gifted
- I AM… flowing with abundance
- I AM… powerful beyond measure
- I AM… love
- I AM… possibility

ACTIVITY:

1. *Sit in a quiet space and meditate.*
2. *Think of what you want to be and visualize I AM statements that resonate with you.*

3. List your top 5 "I AM" statements.

4. Put each I AM statement on a sticky note and post on your bathroom mirror or a place that you view every day.

5. Repeat your I AM affirmation each morning to yourself for 21 days.

We become what we believe is true about ourselves. A vast majority of people are oblivious to this treasure we have at the tip of our tongue. Your beliefs have to vibrationally match your desire. Say it like you mean it! If you don't believe what you have asked for is possible or that you deserve it, then you will begin to repel what you have asked to manifest.

In light of our innate gift of Divine Manifestation, we must also realize that there exists a delicate balance between Source's intentions for our lives and our own personal intentions. We are co-creators of our reality with Source. Therefore, we must never attempt to be adamant that our intentions have to manifest exactly how we want them to, but rather we should enter into a space of allowance and receptivity of what is best for our Spiritual growth and evolution.

Abraham Hicks, the author of the book *The Law of Attraction*, teaches that in order to manifest, one must visualize and get into the vibrational resonance of that which you desire. To do so, you must pay attention to your feelings. To get into positive feelings, you must raise your vibration. Next is to feel good about what is to come, as if it is already there. Your feelings drive the Universe to match your desires to your feelings and belief about what you want, thus magnetizing your desires to you with greater speed.

LUNAR AMPLIFICATION OF MANIFESTATION

You can amplify your manifesting power by taking advantage of the intense energies of the Full Moon and New Moon. The New Moon is the perfect time to plant the seeds of your intentions. It requires a thoughtful process of exactly what you want to manifest. This is similar to planting a seed in an oasis of fertile ground. The New Moon is used for setting intentions (your seed), and the energy of the waxing phases is used for incremental alignment and inspired action towards bringing your intentions into fruition. You should look forward to your intentions, or at least a part of your intentions, to be manifested by the peak of the Full moon. [Source: Numerology.com]

You should continue to reflect, course correct and release what doesn't serve you into the waning phases of the moon. Manifestation on the Full Moon is so incredibly powerful because of the union of the sun's masculine energy and the moon's feminine energy on either side of the earth. This happens when the earth is positioned directly between the sun and the moon and aligned in a straight line. This creates a powerful magnetic energetic field that envelops the earth at this time. When harnessed correctly, this powerful energy can help fast track your intentions into quick manifestation.

6

Total Wellbeing

"I want to know what sustains you from the inside when all else falls away."

—**Oriah Mountain Dreamer**
from "The Invitation"

With recent challenges to our societal norms, there has been a global return to what *really* matters—the well-being of Self, family and community.

Our wellbeing has been neglected the past few decades. Everything is moving rapidly. People are working harder than they've ever worked in prior generations. There is not enough time set aside for rest. Companies are pushing their employees for maximum output and less time for vacation.

In the entire world, American Corporations have among the shortest vacation times set aside for their employees. On average, an American has approximately 17 vacation days for the entire year. Think about that. Three weeks to recover out of 52 weeks of work. This is a mere five percent of the year provided for rest and recovery time.

Other countries, like France, have an average of 30 paid vacation days. This is the norm. It's time for us to really take a good look at how we treat ourselves. Families need time to bond with each other. Parents also need time to spend with their children to raise them the right way. As we know, a healthy and stable family is the foundation of a healthy community. A healthy community is the foundation of a healthy nation. A healthy nation is the foundation of a healthy planet.

COVID-19 has taken the world by storm. It is, however, a blessing in disguise to our planet. This is because it has caused a huge evolution of consciousness on the planet and a return to Self.

The Information Age of the twentieth century has caused us to overwork ourselves – constantly being "on" around the clock. The health of employees has been sacrificed for big stock market gains and large corporate profits. With the need for Corporations to compete in the global economy and provide shareholders with the profits they desire, businesses have had to stay competitive in order to remain in business. Immune systems have become compromised with workers clocking in excessive work hours with little to no rest.

Because the Self has been neglected, people have begun to fall sick in spite of healthcare in the United States becoming more accessible, advanced, and cutting-edge. Anxiety and depression have become more widespread. This has led to a rise in drug abuse, alcohol abuse, food addictions, premature aging and early onset of diseases that normally happen when one is older, such as hypertension and cancer.

Prior to COVID-19, there was a slow shift of mainstream focus to self-care, mental health and holistic wellbeing. However, the emergence of COVID-19, has caused a great acceleration of this shift and a more rapid global elevation of consciousness of our planet. It has brought unprecedented upheaval in the way we live our lives. However, we have the opportunity to realize ourselves as global citizens and loving agents of change. We can either get caught up in the chaos of our world or choose to center ourselves in a calm and steady manner, moving towards a place of possibility and gratitude instead of fear and panic. There is Divine timing at work here, and you have a special role to play for a purpose that is bigger than you and I.

There is a lot of talk now about holistic wellness or integrative medicine. But it is not a new way of thinking about health. Ayurvedic medicine originated in India around 7,000 years ago with the philosophy that perfect health is achieved from a balance of the Mind, Body and Spirit. We remain healthy if we retain this balance. Illness is caused when there is an imbalance in Mind, Body and/or Spirit. When we make bad choices in diet, exercise or relationships, we have the potential to create physical, mental or Spiritual imbalances. These imbalances cause a lack of harmony and make us more susceptible to disease. When we come back into balance, we experience better health.

Total wellbeing is the balance or harmony of the Mind, Body and Spirit. You should always keep all three parts in balance for optimal wellness.

Diagram 16: *Hierarchy of Mind, Body & Spirit*

Body: This is our physical Body.

Mind: This is our mental state.

Spirit: This is your higher Self and Divine connection to Source.

WAYS TO FEED THE BODY, MIND AND SPIRIT

Spirit: The way to feed the Spirit is through daily Spiritual practices (like prayer and meditation). This is what you lean on in the worst of times, when your back is against the wall. This is what will renew you and keep you going.

Mind: The way to feed the Mind is through daily inspirational media (audio, video, text). These help you to take the right perspective on life and have you come into a greater understanding of Self.

Body: The way to feed the Body is through daily balanced nutrition and exercise.

Diagram 17: *Expanded Hierarchy of Mind, Body & Spirit*

MIND-BODY-SPIRIT Wellness Morning Routine

ACTIVITY

1. *Every night before you go to bed, write down your to-do list for the next day.*

2. *Number each item based on the priority level of each task.*

3. *Highlight the top three things you need to do for the day to make it a productive day for you.*

When you wake up each morning, practice taking care of your Mind, Body and Spirit.

ACTIVITY:

For the Spirit:

Begin the day with your Spiritual practice as discussed earlier in this book. Say or listen to prayers or songs that you resonate with. One of my favorites is a song "The Most High One" by Londrelle featuring Lalah Delia.

The Most High One

I surrender to that which is more Divine than myself
Bigger than myself
More aware than myself
Surround me and surround my thoughts
Protect me in all directions
Elevate my self-awareness as I now align
to the highest awareness that is yours.
With this awareness I welcome in the experience
Of high vibrational energy, opportunity and love.
I welcome in Divine peace, balance and mindfulness.
Enter in my thoughts, my Spirit, my Body, my emotions and my Soul.
Enter in my relationships, my plans,
My encounters, my home, my habits, my goals.
Each day guide me, protect me
Strengthen me, fortify me, enlighten me, cover me
Purge my reality of all that does not serve my highest good
I welcome your Supreme presence
And all that is Divine to enter in
You are the sacred one and my Body is a temple

Preserve me, nourish me, fuel me
Charge me up and dwell in my temple daily
I will honor you there and on my journey everywhere
Thank you for your daily provisions,
Guidance and blessings
Thank you for the Divine angels you have
Watching over me, guiding me and protecting me
You are the light
The light that shines in me, around me and through me.
I give thanks and praise to you and for you
The most High One...
And so it is

Sit in silence and meditate. State your intentions for what you desire your day to be.

For the Mind:

Lay a solid foundation for your mind. This can be done with inspirational or motivational media, such as music, a video, or a book or prayer reading. My favorite songs, which are part of my mantras, are "Already Here" and "Surrender" by Srikala. This helps to reprogram my mind to one of abundance. I start my day in bliss and believe anything and everything is possible. I have a free playlist on Spotify called "The Spirit of a Goddess" that are all motivational songs you can listen to at any time. I constantly update this playlist with new songs that speak to my Soul.

For the Body:

> Begin your day with eight ounces of lemon water, followed by a light, healthy and balanced breakfast. Don't forget to add colorful fruits to your breakfast. A multi-grain or oat cereal with strawberries, banana, blueberries, and almond milk topped with a drizzle of honey or agave makes for a light but nutritious breakfast. Next, take a brisk walk outdoors for 20-30 minutes each day. You can also workout indoors during the colder months for the same amount of time. Exercise and nutrition boost your immune system and keep it strong enough to fight disease.

Now, with your Mind, Body and Spirit set up right, and your to-do list in hand, you are ready to begin your day, starting within the intention you set for the day.

The Mind-Body-Spirit Wellness Morning Routine should happen daily. If you do it even for one day, you will notice a huge sense of energy and clarity that carries into the rest of the day. You will feel a great sense of accomplishment at the end of the day, when you knock out even just a few things on your to-do list.

A healthy Spirit governs the Mind. The characteristics of a healthy Spirit are love, joy, peace, patience, kindness, goodness, faithfulness, gentleness and self-control. When you have a healthy Spirit, you will have the gifts of Spiritual discernment (deeper sense of right and wrong), peace of Mind and revelation or Spiritual downloads.

A FEW MORE RESOURCES

There are many other tools and resources available to help you create a healthy Self. Here are some that I recommend.

Personal Development

For a well-balanced mental perspective of yourself and the world around you, I highly recommend you attend a reputable program such as *The Landmark Forum*, which can give you an empowering perspective on how to show up in the world as the best version of you. It has made a huge difference in my life and for hundreds of thousands of people across the world with its highly acclaimed curriculum.

Sacred Adornment

Sacred adornment is the art of dressing for your Spirit. Every time you honor the sacred beauty within you, it is a form of prayer and a show of reverence to the Creator for making such a beautiful gift as you. We, therefore, should be iintentional about what we wear on our sacred Temple Body. Your external presentation is an expression of the inner beauty that resides within you. There is only one you, and there will only be one of you for all of eternity. Therefore, celebrate your uniqueness, Goddessness and magnificent beauty.

I created an offering for Goddesses from all walks of life where I offer beautiful adornment pieces for your Temple Body and a treasure trove of eclectic items, like Goddess crowns and more. You can access these unique pieces on TkdCollective.com.

My Personal Downloads

In my moments of silence and meditation, there are some downloads I've received that I'd like to share with you:

- Death is not something bad, and, therefore, should not be feared.

- When someone dies, do not wallow in sorrow, mourning their loss. Rather, celebrate their life, for they do not belong to you.

    They belong to the Creator. They have completed their agreed upon time of service on this earth and have returned home to the Creator. No matter their manner of departure, try your best to give thanks for the good times they spent with you on this earth. This is how you honor them.

- The salvation of Black people lies in Africa. All Black people must connect back to the African continent.

7

Leadership

"Being a Leader doesn't mean getting up on a podium and speaking to thousands of people. It is in the small things you do each day."

Leadership is all about service to others and leaving the world better than we met it. True Leaders are Creators. They are the ones who step outside the box and take a leap of faith, blazing the path for others to follow behind them. They are the ones who take charge and are proactive in finding answers rather than simply complaining about the status quo. They are the Visionaries, Creatives, Entrepreneurs and Activists. What all these roles have in common is that they *create change*. Leaders are, in essence, change-makers. They make up about just 10 percent of the population. The remaining 90 percent of the earth's population is willing to be led. People are looking for leaders to tell them what to do, what to say, who to be. Just look at the political and social landscape and you can see it for yourself.

Not everyone is built to be a leader of the people; however, you can be a leader of yourself. You can lead in your own small way and still make a difference in people's lives and the world.

What's most important is being a Leader of your own Self—Mind, Body and Spirit. This starts with curiosity, Self-awareness and Self-Discovery. This begins with studying yourself and knowing yourself. You know what types of things bring you joy, what your specific gifts are, what turns you off, what you want in an ideal mate, what yourcore values are, your ideal career, your ideal location to retire to, your ideal hour of rest and so on. You should know what type of activities you need to do to reset your Mind, Body and Spirit like the back of your hand.

Leadership of one's Mind, Body and Spirit culminates in Self-Mastery. This is when discipline, integrity, patience, belief, sacrifice, curiosity, grit, persistence and a strong work ethic ultimately leads to success in all aspects of your life.

8

Relationships

When we think of relationships, the most important relationship is the one you have with yourself. In order to have a relationship with yourself, you have to get to know who you are. When you know who you are, you know your likes and dislikes, what you are attracted to and what repulses you. Only when you have a deep knowledge of Self are you able to set limits in a relationship. This is because knowledge of Self is the path to Self-Love. When you truly love yourself, you are less likely to tolerate abuse.

The reason why relationships can be hard for most people is because we have no control over other people's behavior towards us. We only have control over ourselves and how we react. When we interact with people, we have to take into account their mood, mental state, upbringing, personality, culture—it can be a lot to consider, especially when dealing with challenging personalities. Therefore, it takes some effort to have a consistently positive, peaceful and drama-free relationship with others. There will be ups and downs, no doubt about that. Things will be said that will be misconstrued. Certain expectations will be left unmet. Feelings will get hurt. This can leave you feeling disappointed and let down.

However, we can consider taking a different approach when it comes to relationships that matter to you. When we deal with people, we have either a positive or negative experience. When things turn sour, it causes us to have a negative impression about the person. This sometimes ends up being our fixed and permanent view of who that person is and how we feel about them, even if they eventually end up turning their life around. We subconsciously rank people in our Mind and tag them with our view of them. For example, we might tag someone as evil, conniving, useless and so on.

If you love someone, you should try your best to avoid taking a fixed, judgmental stance against that person. We sometimes use certain harsh words to describe our former friends, partners or spouses. If you remain stuck in this negative viewpoint of your mate, you end up mentally boxing them into the boundaries of who you say they are.

What we don't realize is that our beliefs causes us to show up in ways that validate and thus perpetuate our existing beliefs of others. This could be in our facial expression, our tone of voice or in our attitude. We show up in ways that is consistent with how we feel about them. This tainted way of being triggers a continuous cycle of manifesting our beliefs about this person into our reality, making it true for us.

Therefore, there continues to be a never-ending toxic dynamic which you don't even realize you are subconsciously triggering, because of your beliefs about this person.

> *We inadvertently partake in toxicity through*
> *our subconscious beliefs about others.*
> —**CHE THE GODDESS**

Once we change this belief, then everything else changes. This is because we make room for the transformation of others and our relationship with them.

Transformation cannot happen where there is no possibility. This is because transformation thrives on possibility. This equates to nurturing your partner into a new possibility—with or without you in the picture. In essence, you always want what's best for your partner ,and take a stand for them in the realization of that possibility.

I realize this may be contrary to modern "progressive" beliefs. As independent women, we are taught that when things turn south in a relationship and the relationship ends, we normalize the bashing of our ex as a way to self-soothe our hurt and pain, as well as emotionally disconnect from the relationship.

May I invite you to consider a new possibility? One where you don't have to be with that person any longer, but you still want the absolute best for your partner. You take a stand for them becoming a better version of themselves, as you would for yourself or your child. It can be very challenging at times, but I must say, it's a very rewarding experience if you see it through. It definitely goes against everything we've been taught about relationships.

Please know that I'm not advocating for you to remain in an unhealthy or toxic relationship. Never that. Instead, I'm simply advocating for you to consider showing up as the best version of yourself and also seeing the other person as the highest version of themselves. If you are in a relationship where you are being abused, please do what's best for you and leave as soon as possible. Send the individual love and healing in your thoughts, from afar.

Pay attention to your emotions

When we are hurt by someone, the first thing that happens to us is we feel emotions. You might feel sad, disappointed, shocked or devastated. Try not to make a major decision based solely on how you feel.

Most importantly, never let your emotions guide you in making major, irreversible decisions. If you do, the more sporadic and unreliable you become. Emotions are just energy in motion; they come and go. They are not permanent. Breathe. Let the energy flow through you. Give yourself some time to process how you are feeling. If you are extremely upset, spend a few days to decompress. Sleep on it. Talk to an elder who is in a well-balanced, long-term, positive relationship to get a different perspective. Then come up with a strategy and follow through on it.

Having healthy relationships is a choice. No matter what you are going through, always try your best to see the lesson in your experiences. Choose to consciously love yourself and the person you are becoming through your growth. Choose love over fear always. Don't ever let your past failed relationships make you give up on love and on yourself. Your ideal Soul Mate is out there waiting for you.

EMPATHIC LISTENING

The best way to connect authentically with one another is by being a good listener. Strive to listen from an empathetic view. Being empathetic means mentally stepping into the other person's world and imagining seeing the world from their eyes and walking in their shoes. You don't have to agree with them, but you can put yourself in the situation to begin to understand why they feel what they feel and think what they think. When you listen from a position of genuine empathy, you allow the other person to feel heard and understood. This calms flared tempers, diffuses unnecessary tension, and leads to a quicker resolution to misunderstandings.

Diagram 18: *Empathic Listening*

Know that people act from their highest level of consciousness. They really are doing the best they know how. Understand this and never take anything personally. People operate from the flawed and broken part of their being at their highest level of Self-Love and Self-compassion. If they were able to operate at a higher level of consciousness, they would.

As a Goddess, life revolves around you and putting yourself first. You must love yourself more than you love anyone else. However, because our world is one of a communal one, in order to be successful with your family life, business or career, it takes relationship building.

Therefore, on a certain level we *do* have to care about other people. We must care for ourselves first, then make time out for other people that we love. Paying attention to another person's words, intonation and Body language tells you a a lot about that person, and their state of being.

A lot of people spend time mid-conversation thinking of their response before the other person has finished speaking, instead of paying attention to what the other person is *really* saying. If you regularly do this, then you miss a whole lot of what's really being said. Also, you are not ever being *fully present* in your conversations.

Let's practice being in the present moment. Allow for a pause to process what you have just heard. Pause. Breathe. Get comfortable with silence. Imagine yourself living in that person's shoes. Understand what it means to be them. Let the conversation flow naturally while being your authentic Self. Then speak your Mind and let your thoughts flow intuitively. No over-compensation. Just being in the moment, sitting with that person and holding space for them to speak their truth. If you need to cry or say nothing at all, then do just that. Just *be* there.

Lastly, have compassion for yourself, your flaws, your imperfections and the mistakes you make. Know you are also doing the best you know how. Be gentle on yourself. Love and accept all of yourself. Only when we love and accept ourselves can we truly love and accept others. It all starts from within us.

> *"People struggle to forgive others because they struggle to forgive themselves."*

I used to hold on to grudges for years at a time and struggled to let things go.

When I dug deep into my Shadow, I learned the reason why I was so hard and unforgiving of others was because I was extremely hard on myself. I kept a mental record of all the things I did wrong and rehashed my past mistakes. Once I learned to forgive myself, then it became easier to forgive others, and then slowly I began to let things go. Part of my Self-Love journey involved listening more closely to my Body and taking the cues it gave me to take care of myself—to rest when I needed to rest; if something hurt, to take care of it in a timely manner and not let it fester, to say no to things that didn't resonate with me and not feel guilty about it.

You can't give to others what you do not have. Only when you are compassionate with yourself can you be compassionate with others. After dealing with chronic illness, extreme fatigue and a miscarriage, I've learned to take it easy on myself and take the cues my Body gives me to rest and recharge.

Your Presence is the gift

You are enough. You do not have to prove anything to anyone. Your presence is the gift. You don't have to be anything other than who you are to provide value or make a difference in other people's lives. Your presence and listening are the gifts. Choose the gift of your authentic Self. People will appreciate, respect and value you for it.

EMOTIONS & FEELINGS

Diagram 19: *The Relationship between Thoughts and Emotions*

When you think a thought, your brain automatically ascribes a meaning to the thought. From that meaning, you experience feelings or emotions about what was said. I discovered that if I am able to intercept my thoughts before my Mind can ascribe a meaning to it, then I can interrupt the automatic emotions and feelings I get resulting from my interpretation. Breakthrough!

You can directly shift your emotions/feelings about most things and stop suffering by using this extremely powerful concept. When you are able to recognize this pattern in yourself and interrupt the cycle, it is a form of enlightenment. It was a breakthrough moment for me when I began to use this method to interrupt negative cycles in my personal life. I went from an *extremely reactive* personality to one that is more in control of my emotions by checking in with my thoughts and my interpretation of what I'm experiencing. This eliminated a lot of unnecessary drama from my life.

For example, if someone you hold in high regard disrespects you for no apparent reason, your immediate reaction is most likely one of shock, then disappointment, sadness, hurt, then finally, anger. You may lash out at the person and possibly get into an argument because you feel disrespected and are hurting inside. However, you can interrupt your pattern of thought immediately by asking yourself, "What does this situation mean about me?" Normally you would say, "It made me feel like I don't matter." But when you know that someone's toxic reaction has everything to do with them and nothing to do with you, the answer to this question should be "Nothing!"

A person's toxic reactions to you are a breakdown of their integrity with themselves to show up as a decent human being in this world. Period. The burden is on them to get back in integrity with themselves, then with you. When you fully get this concept, you are able to walk away calmly without even uttering a word. Never let anyone throw you off balance and get you off your throne. As a Goddess, you should strive to remain calm and be fully in control of your words and actions, even when provoked. When you allow someone to throw you out of character, you give up your power. When you remain calm and centered, you stay in your power.

Stick to the facts about the matter

We are emotional beings. This is part of our natural Divine Feminine traits. This is an asset, however sometimes it can work against us if we let our emotions run wild. When there is a breakdown in a relationship, a way to avoid unnecessary conflict is to try as much as possible to stick to the facts about the matter—no opinions, no emotions, no judgment. Just the facts.

It is the *story* we add to the *facts* about the matter that leads to the hurt, pain and drama. A *story* is basically our interpretation or the version "in our head" of what happened, not the actual facts of what occurred.

Your story will normally paint you as the victim, because this is simply how we tell stories, and that's how it goes. No one wants to tell a story and paint themselves out to be the bad guy. Instead, we escape into this rabbit hole of painting ourselves as the victim of the story and then enroll everyone else into feeling sorry for us.

This is why we should try to avoid leaning on stories because in every story, there are *characters* in that story and whenever you tell the story, you will feel the need to continue to remain in character as the *victim* instead of staying in your power and rising above the situation.

When something goes wrong, ask yourself, "What are the facts? What actually happened?" Do not focus on your perception or interpretation of what happened. Emotions aside, stick to the facts, and tackle them one at a time. This will save you from so much unnecessary drama.

Before I learned about sticking to the facts of the matter, I would frequently be embroiled in drama. Arguments would explode, doubling, tripling and quadrupling in size. Everyone and anyone would be pulled in to hear my side of the story. Now that I stick to the facts about the matter, my life has been a lot more drama-free.

BREAKDOWNS IN RELATIONSHIPS

Relationships require effort and intention. A relationship takes commitment from both sides to make it work. Even though two people may appear to have a perfect relationship, this does not exist in reality. Every relationship has its own unique challenges.

Breakdowns are guaranteed to happen. Sometimes we think the perfect relationship should not have a breakdown. However, in reality, breakdowns occur even in healthy, well-balanced relationships. Therefore, we should welcome breakdowns in relationships instead of avoiding or resisting them. This is because breakdowns present both parties with an opportunity to uncover what is missing in the relationship. Welcoming and dealing with breakdowns head-on allow you to discover what's missing, fill the gap, and strengthen your relationship. Breakdowns also allow for a better understanding and appreciation of each other.

Here's what to do when a breakdown occurs:

- Discover what the facts are that caused the breakdown.
- Describe what happened step-by-step (facts only).
- Step into the other person's world, to fully understand the breakdown from their point of view and reasoning behind what they did or said.

- Take full responsibility for the part you played in the breakdown.
- Lastly, commit to a new possibility that creates a higher commitment that transcends the breakdown that just occurred to build an even stronger relationship.

LOVE AND SEX

Sometimes we equate love to sex. This is so not true. Love is not always about sex. It's really the intimacy we yearn for. We yearn to be touched, held, admired and appreciated. We yearn to be understood and acknowledged. That's what we are really craving. This is what is missing in most relationships. When the intimacy leaves, the sex disappears. When the intimacy returns, then the sex will naturally follow. Work on going on dates with your partner and engage in fun activities together—just the two of you. This helps to rekindle the intimacy in your relationship.

If you are single, fight the urge to seek out sex as a means of filling a void in your life—whether it be loneliness, lack of love or attention or just not feeling worthy. Write down the top five things you seek in a mate that are non-negotiable. When you meet someone you may be romantically interested in and want to explore things further, mentally go through your top five priorities before you invest in a long-term relationship. Look to become friends first. This person might make a good friend and bring something of value into your life, but they may not make an ideal romantic partner. A romantic relationship built on a foundation of true friendship will stand the test of time. Take the time to get to know each other and learn about your likes and dislikes. Develop a true understanding, mutual respect and appreciation for each other. When you invest in a relationship with the right partner, you reap the rewards of your commitment. You get an also equally committed partner who will ride with you through thick and thin. When you date many people at the same time, you spread yourself thin, and at the end of the day, you have nothing to show for it. Multiple partners cause multiple problems and only digs you into a deeper abyss of even more sadness, loneliness and ultimately regret.

9

Struggle Is Only a Season

"I want to know if you can sit with pain—mine or your own without moving to hide it or fade it or fix it."

Oriah Mountain Dreamer
—from "The Invitation"

Life is like a rollercoaster ride. There will be ups and downs. With the downs, you will have times when you struggle to find the meaning behind your pain or to just simply overcome the challenges in front of you.

Struggle is not a bad thing. It's simply an opportunity for growth. The discomfort and pain you feel is the pressure needed to push you towards your transformation—perfectly and divinely prepared for you to elevate to a higher level of consciousness.

When confronted with hard times, push through. Do not make a permanent decision out of a temporary situation. Push through! Ask yourself, "What's the lesson I need to learn from this?" Who do I need to become in order to thrive in this situation? What characteristics/attributes do I need to embody to be the highest version of myself in this situation?"

Then embody these qualities—be more loving, patient, forgiving, and kind; have more self-control and be better prepared. Then just simply *be* that person and master your becoming. In life, the Universe presents you with two choices: evolve or repeat. Learn the lesson and become better, stronger and wiser in mastering the lesson to prepare for your next level of evolution. If the lesson is not fully learned, the lesson keeps repeating itself until you master it, and then you rise above it. It's like a fish and bait. The fish is presented with yummy bait, but if the fish swallows the bait, it will lose its life. If the fish learns to swim around the bait, no matter how yummy it looks, then it learned the lesson of not getting trapped by enticing, dangerous circumstances. Now, it can move on to the next lesson ahead.

It's similar to a video game where a player keeps losing their life in a round, until they learn how to overcome what keeps tripping them up on that level, and once they have successfully learned their lesson allowing them to make it to the end of that round, then they are presented with their next higher level of challenge. If they don't learn their lesson, the level keeps repeating itself. Same with life.

Difficulties present opportunities for growth

With difficulties come opportunities for growth and transformation. Don't dwell on why things didn't work out, why your partner left, why you got fired from the job, why so-and-so doesn't love you anymore, why your loved one has a terminal illness, why you have a chronic illness or a lifelong disability, and so on. Ask yourself, "What is the highest version of myself I need to be to get the best out of this situation?" Then embody that quality.

Suicide is a tough subject, but I feel the need to touch on it because of the times we are living in. Suicide is a bad idea on a Soul level.

There have been numerous accounts from Spiritual mediums who communicated with Spirits who committed suicide. They describe these Souls as having a weight, a heaviness and immense sorrow around them in the Spiritual realm. They communicate that they thought their suicide would free them from the pain they were going through and they would rest eternally. However, this was not the case. What they didn't realize was that by committing suicide you only get rid of your Body.

The psychological and emotional distress you had prior to committing suicide still remains with you after death, and you still have to work through it. Most Spirits who take their own life communicate feeling regret, immense sorrow and an unworthiness to rise up to the higher realms of unconditional love. They also witness their family grieve for them and watch all the pain, loss and heartache they caused to their loved ones. They end up feeling guilty and regretting taking their own lives.

It is a breach of your Soul contract to take your life. Prior to your birth, your Soul agreed to learn certain life lessons in order to ascend to a higher level of consciousness; however, you terminated the contract ahead of your agreed-upon time, so you end up in a contractual deficit. The best thing to do, as tough as it is, is to ride it out. Do the best you can to make the best of your circumstances. Struggle really is a season—it's temporary. Pain is not eternal. It is temporary. There is a start date and -an end date. Just like there is darkness at night and then morning breaks and sunlight appears like clockwork, your darkness will always eventually subside and give way to sunshine to light up your life.

Ask Source for answers to the questions you are seeking. Let Source speak to you in the silence of your thoughts and reflections. Stay silent and meditate. Source speaks through our subconsciousness. Write down the visions, ideas, suggestions or inspirations coming through to you. We have all the answers we are seeking, if only we just ask the question.

You have been created with everything you need to thrive. Because you are always connected to Source, you have constant access to Divine, infinite wisdom, knowledge and guidance.

AVOIDING CYNICISM AND RESIGNATION

It is easy to fall into the trap of resignation and sadness with certain overwhelming circumstances—a death in the family, a chronic disease, extreme fatigue, or mental illness, for example. Accepting things we cannot change gives us peace of Mind. Make beauty out of the ashes. This means make the best out of a bad situation. Create a home that rises up to greet you when you walk in…scented candles, soothing music, green plants, etc. Simplicity is best. A clean and inviting home soothes the senses and becomes your source of refuge in challenging and chaotic times.

When faced with struggle:

- Feel the pain, but push through. Don't let it overwhelm you and take you down. Express gratitude in advance for the victory over the struggle and believe the battle has already been won. Visualize what the battle being won looks like—good health, a successful career, a successful marriage, a profitable business, your children turning out okay or a divorce battle settled amicably.

- Next, embody who you need to be to overcome that struggle—patient, loving, nurturing, etc. Stay in action! Do the things you have in your power to get you back on solid ground. Stay in communication with others—your family, your friends. Take a walk outside and get some fresh air. Go for a drive to change your scenery. Set up your remote workstation in a different part of the house, on your balcony with a view, patio or in your backyard garden to switch up the monotony in your daily routines and create a blissful backdrop.

- Lastly, have faith that no struggle is permanent. Every struggle has a start and end date, just like the seasons. It will eventually pass, and the sun will come out and shine over you again.

For the things you cannot change, such as terminal illness, move towards acceptance and gratitude for bringing that beautiful Soul into contact with you, for the joys that person brought into your life and the good times you got to share together. This will usher in some peace of Mind. It really helped me a lot when my sister-in-law was passing away from cancer.

We've talked about how to handle hard issues like the death of a loved one. Now let's talk about softer issues, those in which your survival or that of a loved one (food, shelter, life) is not at risk. Consider relationship issues such as breakups, divorce or falling out with a family member or close friend. In a case like this, you want to take some time to yourself to understand why the relationship fell apart. What role did you play? What role did others play? What is the lesson? Is it a falling out that was meant to be with you both simply growing apart? Is it a toxic or non-serving relationship that had to end? Is this for your betterment? If so, learn to be still and sit with the pain. Feel the grief, the hurt and the loss. Accept the loss, then seek healing. Please know that not all relationships are meant to last a lifetime. Some Soul contracts with people you come across and build a friendship with are only for a specific time in your life. Once it has served its purpose, then the contract has been met. There is nothing left to do or say. It is okay to move on and be open to receiving new blessings, people and opportunities coming your way.

In summary, when you deal with tragedy, proceed with gratitude and acceptance. Cry through the hurt and pain. Allow your tears to flow, as they are cathartic and helps to relieve sadness and anxiety. Research shows that shedding tears is not only self-soothing, but it also releases oxytocin and endorphins. These chemicals ease both physical and emotional pain.

Movement also helps to relieve stress. Move your Body and dance through your pain. Seek counsel by talking through your grief with a trusted friend, family member, therapist or counselor for guidance and moral support. When we share what we are going through with others, they provide us with perspective. Talking through your issues also helps to ease the stress of dealing with your problems alone.

When you sit with the pain and don't try to avoid it or hide from it, you program yourself to not repeat the cycle. This is because with pain, a hard lesson is fully learned and imbibed. Toxic relationships are revealed so you can take the hit, excise them from your life, and move on from them. If the lesson is not learned, the cycle continues to repeat itself until you truly *get* the lesson.

Picture yourself going through the "fire" and making a U-turn midway to come back around to your starting position and then back through the fire once again. That's the definition of insanity if you ask me. But most of us do that to ourselves over and over again. Basically, we are on a *mistakes on repeat* cycle. Sometimes, that's what it really takes to be truly *done* with a certain something or someone. If you are not done with a situation, life will continue to bring you back to it so you can fully *get* the lesson and stay the hell away from the fire.

When you are facing challenging times, how will you handle it going forward? Remember, your thoughts create your reality, so focus on what makes you happy. Express gratitude to Source, not just for the good times, but also for the struggles and setbacks. Difficult times present you with your most valuable and most transformative lessons. Trust the Divine path you are on, and take pride in your ability to evolve.

> *"...[T]he non-permanent appearance of happiness and distress, and their disappearance in due course, are like the appearance and disappearance of winter and summer seasons. They arise from a sense of perception...and one must learn to tolerate them without being disturbed."*
>
> —THE BHAGAVAD GITA 2:14

Lastly, tough times are temporary. Like anything temporary, there is always a beginning date and an end date. They come and they go, just like the seasons. When you go through hard times, you persevere with the belief that better days are on the way. And just like winter, tough times melt away and the sun comes out to shine bright over you again.

10

Anxiety and Depression

When the Body is neglected, it groans and objects by manner of pain, discomfort or physical illness. When the Mind and Spirit are neglected, it objects by manner of anxiety and sometimes even depression. Total wellness comes from having Mind, Body and Spirit properly cared for and in balance.

Certain chronic conditions can be reversible with a healthy and balanced diet incorporating raw fruits and vegetables and regular exercise. People look far and wide searching for a secret formula that can cure illness, but then are forced to come back to the basic tried and true way of living a healthy life—diet and exercise.

Mental health has gotten more attention lately, as a number of high-profile celebrities have given voice to this important issue. Lady Gaga shared, "I openly admit to having battled depression and anxiety and I think a lot of people do. I think it's better when we all say: 'Cheers!' and 'fess up to it.'"

Kerry Washington spoke with *Glamour* magazine in 2015 of her struggles by saying "…I think it's really important to take the stigma away from mental health. … My brain and my heart are really important to me. I don't know why I wouldn't seek help to have those things be as healthy as my teeth. I go to the dentist. So why wouldn't I go to a shrink?"

The same way we go to a doctor when we break a bone is the same way we should see a doctor if we have anxiety or depression. It is an illness, and even though sometimes it doesn't present in a tangible way, it is equally important as a physical ailment. Unfortunately, it gets swept under the carpet and then ends up taking you down when you least expect it.

Meditation and Mindfulness are some ways to combat anxiety and depression. Exercise and nutrition also are very helpful in keeping stress and anxiety in check. For moderate to severe anxiety, a psychiatrist can prescribe a variety of medications that can help. Please discuss with a trusted physician to see what works best for you.

Anxiety can present itself as extreme fatigue, tightness in the back muscles, shortness of breath, a feeling of being stressed out, difficulty falling asleep, foggy brain and even some memory loss. With anxiety, you can sleep for ten hours a day and still feel tired.

Anxiety and Depression

You also may notice you have difficulty paying attention in meetings or following a lengthy or detailed conversation. Anxiety can go easily undetected because it doesn't always present itself as the more obvious panic attacks. It can creep up on you slowly until it manifests as physical pain.

Sometimes people are ashamed of sharing with others that they have anxiety or depression for fear of being judged or stigmatized. Some end up abusing food, alcohol, drugs or sex to help them cope with their symptoms. People have been self-medicating for decades with marijuana just to get by. They learn how to cope and stay under the radar. They have high-profile jobs and are high achievers. Others are not even aware that they have anxiety or depression and have found unhealthy ways to get by. Many are oblivious to the fact that there are actually great resources out there to significantly improve quality of life and dramatically lessen symptoms.

Meditation and Mindfulness are practices that you can incorporate to manage anxiety. Meditation guru and Spiritual coach Deepak Chopra describes anxiety as one living in the past or the future. Even though this doesn't account for all cases of anxiety, some people get stressed out just by worrying over things that happened in the past or things they fear might happen in the future. They are not living in the present moment. Mindfulness is the practice of living in the present moment, where you practice being fully present. It allows you to be aware of where you are, what you are doing, and not be overly reactive or overwhelmed by what's going on around you. Meditation and yoga are some examples of Mindfulness practices. Meditation is a practice of quieting or calming the Mind. You can calm your Mind down by following the Meditation practices described in Chapter 2.

Anxiety and/or depression can be chronic, or they can be acute conditions caused by certain temporary circumstances or events. Some women suffer temporarily from post-partum depression after giving birth. Other women suffer from chronic depression that lasts a lifetime.

If you suspect you have anxiety that is causing a major degradation of your wellbeing or you are experiencing depression that lasts over a week, please immediately talk to your doctor and get proper medical help. Uncontrolled anxiety or depression can lead to food addictions, drug addictions and, even worse, suicide. Take it seriously and get the help you need or for your loved one. You are so worth it.

Use meditation, yoga and daily exercise to help you better deal with stress. Incorporate dark green, leafy vegetables into your daily diet. Also incorporate a colorful mix of fruits and vegetables with every meal—the more color, the more variety of vitamins and minerals are present in your food, so have fun with it and mix it up a bit.

Now, if you are anything like me, you are super busy and don't have a lot of downtime to buy and prep vegetables and fruits for your daily consumption. What I do instead is use a healthy fruit smoothie delivery service called Daily Harvest. Their fruit and vegetable smoothies taste absolutely delicious, even better than a lot of the top smoothie brick-and-mortar store brands out there. I also buy fresh produce and assemble my own salads and make healthy meals incorporating fish, which also help me feel great.

Seafood is high is omega-3 fatty acids, which helps in fighting anxiety and depression. Dark chocolate also helps in fighting mild depression as it stimulates the production of endorphins, which are chemicals in the brain that create feelings of pleasure. It contains serotonin which elevates the mood. Look for dark chocolate that's low in sugar. It is best to indulge in dark chocolate in moderation. It can be too much of a good thing!

What I personally want to share with you is that, whether you have anxiety or depression, it is nothing to feel ashamed about. The discomfort you feel is your Body letting you know that it is working as designed and signaling you to rest and recharge.

A lot of people who have anxiety are Empaths, as they possess enhanced sensory perceptions. Empaths are natural healers and some even have psychic gifts like Clairvoyance (intuitive vision), Claircognizance (intuitive knowing) and Clairsentience (intuitive feeling).

People who battle depression are very compassionate and caring individuals. Their pain helps them become naturally more sensitive and understanding of other people's pain. They make great caregivers, doctors, nurses and healers. Your gifts are much needed, especially in today's world of great pain, suffering, sickness and chaos.

11

Spirit

When Spirit is infinite and exists everywhere. The restrictions of space and time that apply to matter have no meaning to the Spirit at all. To fully understand and have an appreciation of the Spirit, we have to take a deeper dive into the details surrounding our existence.

We are made in the image and likeness of the Creator and, therefore, exist as a Trinity. Our Trinity is our Spirit, Soul and Body. Our Inner Self consists of our Soul and Spirit. Our Outer Self consists of our physical Body.

The Soul is our unique identity or personality. The Spirit is a part of our Inner Self that is vessel that allows energy to take residence within;

Spirit

it is in the Spirit that we can communicate with the Divine Source of all creation.

Diagram 20: *Inner & Outer Self*

When you die, your Inner Self—Soul and Spirit in unison—leave your physical Body, transition into the Spiritual realm and continue on in its infinite existence. Your Inner Self's occupation within your physical Body is what gives your physical Body its life, vitality and personality.

You are a Spiritual being temporarily existing in a physical Body on this planet for a limited amount of time. You have a purpose to fulfill on this earth. If you do not fulfill your Spiritual purpose on this earth, there is something that becomes missing in the Spiritual world.

You live in a world of infinite abundance and you are the Creator of your reality and the master of your fate. You are not a victim of the circumstances around you but the author of your destiny. You have the power of free will and the gift of Divine Manifestation to choose how you want to live your life and who you want to be.

Diagram 21: *Expanded Diagram of Body, Soul and Spirit*

We have the Universe at our beck and call, and whatever it is that we ask for, the Universe conspires to bring our desires into fruition. Whoever you believe you are is who you become. We have a ton of infinite power at our disposal. We have infinite possibilities at our fingertips and on the tip of our tongue, waiting to be released and activated. We haven't even scratched the surface of what is possible in our lives. We need to be brave to take the step forward and live as our highest selves, step into our Divine birthright and live as the most powerful possible version of ourselves.

When we connect to Source energy, then we are able to tap into a peace-of-mind and fulfillment that defies all human understanding.

We will continue to search everywhere for peace of Mind. However, we will find no true, fully restorative, lasting peace until we seek and find it in ourselves. The Soul is renewed with Self-affirmative words. It is likened to taking a Spiritual bath every time our Soul feels worn out and beat down by the trials and tribulations of life. It allows our Mind, will and conscience to be more receptive to doing what is righteous, just, loving, kind and true.

As we transition from of one era into the end, you must use your Spirit of discernment to know truth from false. Always go back to the 42 Laws of Maat or the 10 commandments for ground rules on how to conduct yourself.

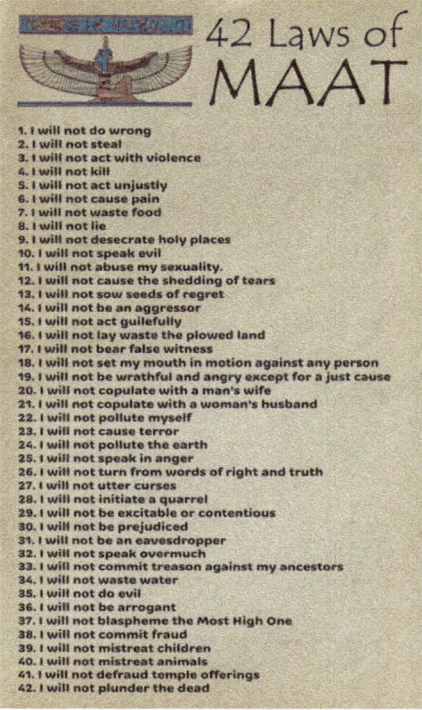

Diagram 22: *The 42 Laws of Maat*

There is a battle that rages between your physical Body and your Spirit over your Soul.

- ⊙ Your Body wants what feels good to your flesh.

- ⊙ Your Spirit wants what is morally right, just and edifying.

- ⊙ Your Spirit tells the Soul to do what benefits it Spiritually; however, the Body tells the Soul to do what feels good to its senses.

- ⊙ Your Soul uses its free will to decide what to do based on the information it's been provided by your Spirit and Body.

Spirit

A battle between *high vibration* versus *low vibration* consistently rages over your Soul while you are on this earth. When you develop a deep Spiritual life, you have a better chance of making decisions that benefit you Spiritually. When you feed into the nature of your physical Body, you will most likely make decisions on what is pleasurable to the Body short-term and not necessarily for your long-term Spiritual benefit.

Your Spirit is your connection to the Divine. You must feed your Spirit daily through spiritual observances, prayer, self-edifying words and engaging in meditative practices. This will strengthen and sharpen your spiritual discernment, which will then guide you towards making better decisions that will ultimately benefit you long term.

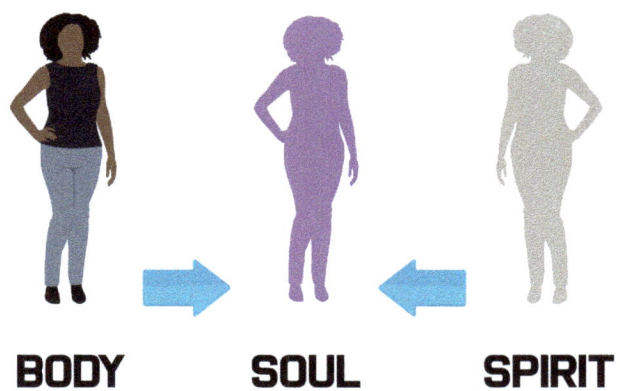

Diagram 23: *Battle between your Body & Spirit over influence of your Soul*

Your Soul logically sits in between your Spirit and your physical Body. Your Spirit is in constant communication with your Soul to get you to do what is in alignment with your highest good. Your Body, on the other hand, wants to do what feels good and is pleasing to the flesh. Hence the Body and Spirit are in constant conflict, providing constant information to your Soul. Your Soul then uses the input provided and makes an informed decision based on your free will, on the best course of action to take based on the input it is provided.

12

Energy

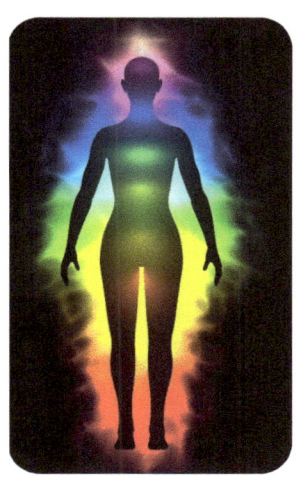

Every living thing has an aura. It is an invisible, magnetic field of energy that surrounds your entire Body. We can sense the auric field of a person when we pick up on their vibe. This is the energy that intuitive people feel and use in their discernment.

Your aura is your first point of contact with the world, and therefore, it can often say more about you than your words can. It's a three-dimensional ellipse that extends above you, beneath you, in front of you, behind you, and to either side. Sometimes your aura extends only inches away from your skin. However, for most people, it tends to expand to about two to three feet away from the surface of the skin.

Now, there are other people who have auras that extend so far out, they fill up an entire room. Similarly, a contracted aura extends just inches away from your skin. This can feel like safety for some people and like anxiety for others.

Energy that comes from the Universal energy field is called *Qi* (pronounced chi) by the Chinese, *chi* by the Igbos in West Africa and *prana* by the Hindus. This energy is what fills up our Body and causes it to be alive and vibrant. Energy is absorbed into your being through natural food, water, raw fruits and vegetables, fruit and vegetable juices, meats, grains, crystals, plants, and the Universe. The energy of the *chi* emits a vibrational frequency as well as bright, vibrant colors within your aura.

Practitioners of Chinese Medicine and Qi Gong have identified various kinds of Qi. These are as follows:

- The Qi that you are born with called Yuan Qi or ancestral Qi
- The Qi that you absorb from food and water called Hou Tain Qi
- The Qi that flows at the surface of the Body called Wei Qi (i.e. the aura)
- The Qi that is held in each organ (e.g. Spleen-Qi, Lung-Qi, Kidney-Qi)
- The Qi that is held within the earth—its trees, flowers, lakes and mountains is called Earth Qi
- The Qi that is held within the Universe is called Universal Qi

  Please note: The above list is by no means exhaustive.

In China, Qi is the foundation of many wellness and healing practices such as Feng Shui, Acupuncture and Qi Gong. Reiki practitioners, also utilize the principles of energy healing to unblock chakras and allow the flow of energy through the chakra junctions of the energetic Body.

Stagnant or imbalanced Qi leads to disease, while free-flowing Qi results in good health. Practitioners of Qi Gong and Feng Shui perceive these energetic imbalances and blockages and apply various techniques to open up the flow of energy within the Body.

The aura is a rainbow-colored energy field usually invisible to the physical eye but can be perceived psychically or subconsciously. Its size is a reflection of your unique personality and makeup.

You can have a large or small aura, depending on whether you have a naturally extroverted or an introverted personality. You have a larger aura when you are aligned with your higher Self and have achieved a high level of consciousness and Spiritual growth. Its color is a reflection of your state of Mind and well-being. When you are experiencing sadness, joy, illness or well-being, your auric color changes to reflect this. Your aura can, therefore, expand, contract or change colors at different moments each day.

Ever notice how some people have such a captivating presence? They'll walk into a room, and everyone notices them. An example is Kobe Bryant. He had a larger-than-life personality, and everyone around him felt it. That's the impact of an extended aura. These people are taking up space, not with their physical bodies, but with their large aura. They are people who have dominant personalities and are usually very charismatic and confident. Gautama Buddha, the Spiritual Leader on whose teachings Buddhism was founded, was said to have an aura that extended over several miles.

When your aura takes up the entire room, you'll feel connected to everyone in the room, and they'll also feel connected to you. Let's say you're speaking in public. You'll want your aura to expand way out. You'll want to feel as if you own the room, and you'll want others to be moved by your presence.

On the opposite end of the spectrum, there are some people who have a naturally occurring contracted aura, and they end up *not* being that memorable. You could have a long conversation with them, and the next time you see them, you find you are re-introducing yourself to them as if you never met. That's a contracted aura! People with a contracted aura are normally extremely introverted and thus are fine with going unnoticed.

only good vibes allowed

Ways to instantly improve your aura

1. Silence rejuvenates your aura. This is why you see Monks often go on silent retreats. Silence helps to calm your Mind and expand your aura.

2. Meditation helps to improve your aura as you quiet the Mind and perform slow breathing exercises. This helps the muscles relax and the aura expand outwards.

3. Spend time in natural sunlight for at least 30 minutes a day, especially if you work in a setting with constant artificial lighting. Artificial lighting drains the aura and sunlight helps to replenish it.

4. Eat raw fruits and vegetables that are brightly colored. It helps to renew your auric field.

5. Keep live flowers, herbs and plants in and around your home. They infuse your aura with that of health and abundance.

6. Engage in gentle movement such as dancing, swimming, walking, and hula hooping, as this helps to shift your auric energies and get it flowing. Your energetic junctions or chakras tend to become stagnant or blocked from the build-up of negative emotions and stress during the day.

7. Avoid using electronic devices for long periods of time, as rays from computers, cell phones, TVs and electronic appliances can deplete the aura.

8. Consider getting a pet. They are great at transferring or overlaying their loving auric energies onto ours. Some great pets to own are adult-friendly dogs and cats.

9. Surround yourself with people who have positive energy. Children (especially babies and toddlers) have a very loving, positive auric field. Being around children can improve the quality of your auric field.

Every living thing carries a field of energy around it. This is because on an atomic level, all things are made up of electrons orbiting around a nucleus. Because we are made up of energy, we have the ability to raise or lower our energy levels or vibrational frequency.

Your aura is connected to the seven energy centers or what in Hinduism is called the *chakras* of the Body. Your aura extends out in seven layers away from the Body—the closest layer being the strongest and the farthest layer being the weakest. The layers of your aura pulsate away from your Body. A healthy aura pulsates a few feet away from the Body.

The chakras are major energetic junctions or energy centers along the Body's central nervous system (or spine) where a number of *nadis*, which are channels or meridians, converge. They are pictured as spinning disks or wheels of energy that run along the spine. The chakra system originated in India between 1500 and 500 BC in the oldest ancient texts called the Vedas and Upanishads. This knowledge migrated to China and was incorporated and harmonized with the Traditional Chinese Medicine (TCM) concepts of the flow of energy.

In light of Hindi and Chinese Medicine philosophies on energy, scientists began investigating the existence of the aura over a hundred years ago. Baron Wilhelm von Richenbach is credited for discovering several properties related to the human energy field that he called the *odic force*. He discovered that it shared similar properties to the electromagnetic field. The odic human energy field was found to be composed of opposite charges, also described as *polarities*. With odic forces, like attracts like. This explains why with people's aura or energy, like attracts like. People on similar energy frequencies attract or magnetize each other. People with opposite frequencies repel each other.

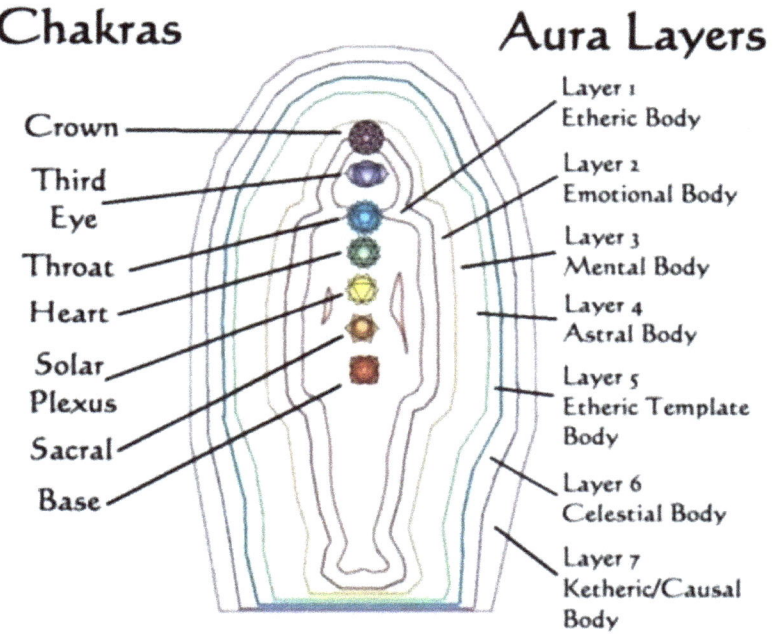

Diagram 25: *The Aura layers*

In 1911, Dr. Walter Kilner examined the aura with a colored filter and a special kind of coal tar. He discovered that the conditions of the aura shifted in reaction to a subject's state of Mind and health.

The aura has been known by many names in many cultures. For example, Christian artists depict Jesus Christ, the Virgin Mary and Saints as surrounded by a halo of light. The aura was discovered to have seven layers varying in depth and size as depicted in Diagram 26.

ENERGY DOESN'T LIE

When you engage in activities that are edifying, they raise your energy or vibrational frequency to that of love, which brings about feelings of joy, peace of Mind and fulfillment. However, when you engage in activities that are toxic, they bring about feelings of disease, sadness, worry, anxiety, anger and self-doubt, which lower your vibrational frequency.

You are responsible for the energy you carry around with you. You have the power to shift your energy when you sense you are in a low vibrational state and raise it to a higher vibration through prayer, meditation, affirmations, movement and other Spiritual practices already discussed in Chapter 2. You also have the power to use nature to ground your energy in order to return back to a state of safety, peacefulness and harmony.

Empaths feel or even absorb other people's energy around them. Empaths end up absorbing feelings such as sadness, joy, anger, pain, angst, and sickness. This is why Empaths tend to suffer from anxiety or depression until they learn to set boundaries and protect their energy.

Not everyone deserves to have access to you

You are responsible for who you have around you and who you allow to have access to you. Avoid people who sap your energy, those who make you feel drained or down after interacting with them. These are known as "energy vampires." This doesn't mean they are bad people. It is just that they are succumbing to the stresses of life and giving in to their own cynicism, fears and doubts. They simply need to work on elevating to a higher level of consciousness, which will help them better work through their issues and raise their vibration.

AURA COLORS

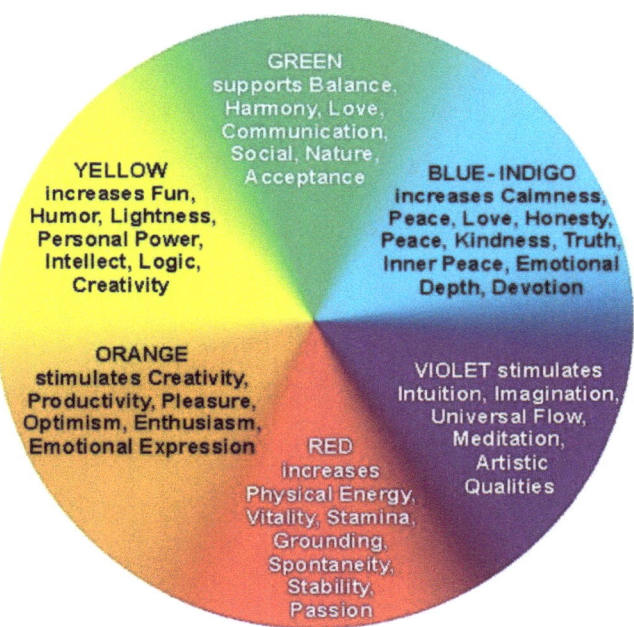

Diagram 26: *The Aura Color Wheel*

Let's get back to talking about aura colors. We mentioned earlier that your aura colors change according to your state of Mind and well-being. Did you know the colors of your aura also indicate the frequency of your energy, thoughts, feelings, mood and state of wellbeing? When your aura radiates brightly, this indicates a state of joy, good health and vitality. Dark, murky and muddled colors can represent negativity, sadness, sickness, sluggishness and general imbalance.

The following list is a great guide, and can be found at: http://annaferraraccio.com/auras.

- **Purple** in your aura shows that you are becoming more Spiritually open and aware.

- **Blue** symbolizes a balanced energy and intuitive abilities. Bright royal blue can indicate clairvoyant skills.

- **Green** is a restorative color that signifies natural healing abilities.

- **Yellow** indicates a playful, inquisitive nature or Spiritual awakening.

- **Orange** is associated with emotions and vitality. Bright orange indicates you are in good health and living life to the fullest.

- **Red** represents action. Dark shades of red suggest self-sufficiency, while cloudy red highlights negative energy and repressed anger.

- **Pink** is the color of the heart and is often visible in the aura when someone is in love.

- **Brown** is the aura color that is associated with fear of the unknown.

- **Grey** represents blocked or stagnant energy, and can also indicate depression or the dark side of your personality.

- **Black** highlights negativity and an unwillingness to forgive.

- **White** auras are rare and are usually only seen surrounding highly Spiritual people who have transcended physical reality.

- **Silver and gold** are aura colors that surround people who have a high Spiritual vibration.

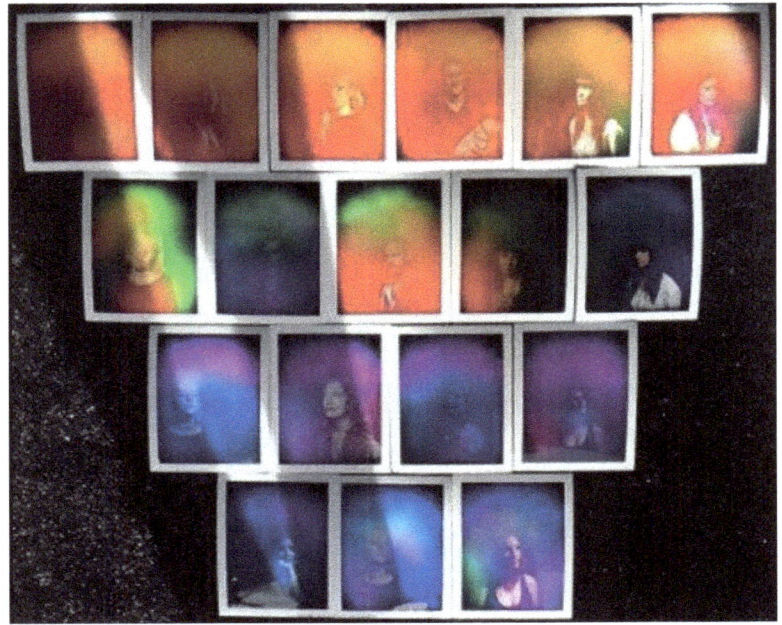

Diagram 27: *Kirlian Photography images of people's aura*

Your aura can be captured by an electromagnetic camera using a method known as Kirlian photography. The aura image captures the most predominant aura colors around the head and shoulders of the subject. Diagram 28 shows aura photographs of various people at a photo studio.

13

The Shadow

Do you know that 95 percent of your thoughts, beliefs and behavior come from your subconscious Mind? Think of your subconscious Mind as an invisible, auto-pilot, GPS engine running in the background of your Mind, navigating you through life, and when you arrive at your destination, you have no idea how you got there. Sound familiar?

As we navigate our relationships and day-to-day life, our conscious Mind checks out and the subconscious Mind runs the show the majority of the time. It drives your beliefs, thoughts, actions and feelings about yourself, others and the world around you.

The Shadow

The Shadow is the *repressed* or *disowned* aspect of our personality that is hidden in our *subconscious Mind*. I use the term *Shadow*, *Shadow Wound*, *Shadow Belief* and *Inner Child Wound* interchangeably in this chapter because these terms essentially all mean the same thing.

The concept of the Shadow has existed for thousands of years with the Shamans and indigenous tribes; however, it was legendary Swiss psychologist Carl Jung who introduced the Shadow concept to the Western world. Jung described the Shadow as being triggered in one's early childhood years by a *projection*. He describes the Shadow as being created the first moment one's parent(s) or someone of authority *projects* themselves on a child, leading them to feel shame and repress the aspect of their personality reprimanded as a survival response.

The birthing of your Shadow happens in your early childhood. New Shadows are formed throughout your teenage and adult life caused by *emotional or psychological trauma.* Some examples are a traumatic rejection, such as a breakup in a relationship, getting fired from a job, divorce or even the sudden death of a loved one. These situations can cause feelings of abandonment, neglect, not being good enough, trust issues or guilt.

Our Shadow Beliefs create energetic cords that attract people into our lives who reinforce our deepest Shadow wound(s). Therefore, our deepest Shadow Beliefs become like an oracle—a self-fulfilling prophecy that reflects back what we subconsciously believe to be true about ourselves.

This is because the Universe is based on frequency, and thoughts are things magnetizing people and situations into our lives that resonate with our given frequency. Even if you are totally unaware that you have a Shadow belief of *not being good enough*, you will still attract people into your life who will affirm this belief. This causes unwanted, toxic, repeated cycles in our lives where we feel we are "*the victim*" and we have no idea why these things keep happening to us. Even when we pick up and move to a different city, state, country or job, we still encounter the *same* issues—*same script, just different faces*. This is why it is so critical for us to uncover and heal our Shadow wounds in order to enable your toxic repeated cycles to begin cease.

This applies not only with our romantic relationships but also with our friendships as well. It takes a subconscious type of *confidence* to go after our dreams, end a toxic relationship and step into a new, positive one. You have to feel worthy.

The setbacks we experience with our *hidden* Shadow beliefs come from the fact that when we reject the unwanted qualities within ourselves, we also unknowingly disown many of our best qualities. These hidden gifts can lie untapped within our Shadow for years, decades and sometimes, sadly, even a lifetime.

It is easier for others to point out your Shadow within you, than for you to do so on yourself. This is because of the elusive nature of the Shadow. It is good at showing up as one thing as a camouflage for something else. For example, feelings of *unworthiness* as a child can show up as perfectionism in adulthood. *Neglect or abandonment wounds* as a child can show up as co-dependency as an adult.

The Shadow

This is why Shadow work done alone (simply journaling) is not nearly as effective as one done by another on you (in a 1-on-1 setting) or in a group setting. This is why I offer 1-on-1 and group coaching in my Shadow to Self-Love Mastery program.

http://shadowtoselfloveacademy.teachable.com

It is critical to uncover your Shadow belief because this is the beginning of doing the work that allows you to eventually transmute and heal.

If you don't know what your Shadow belief is and are wondering what it is, I created this 60-minute online quiz to help you identify it.

http://myinnerchildwoundquiz.netlify.app

The Shadow to Self-Love Methodology

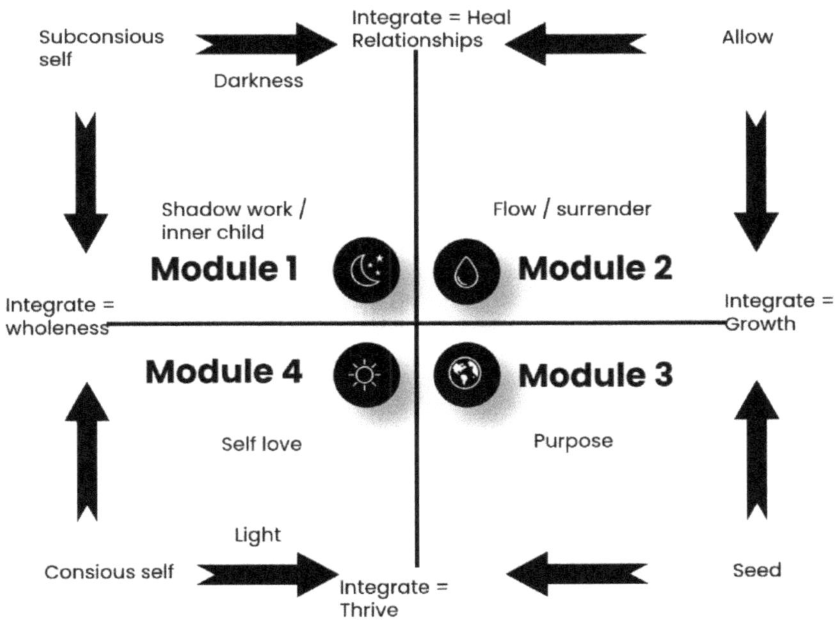

Diagram 28: *The Shadow to Self-Love Grid*

I created the *Shadow to Self-Love Grid*™ above as a visual means of integrating various aspects of ourselves—moon, sun, water and earth energies to experience wholeness, heal our relationships, fulfill our Purpose and thrive. Below is a quick description of this grid.

With respect to your Purpose, when you consciously shed light on your Purpose, you begin to identify and birth the gifts within you in order to thrive.

By simply showing up in our natural Divine Feminine state, we enter into a state of *surrender* rather than *forcing or chasing*. When we invite this Divine flow into our subconsciousness, we begin to heal our relationships.

When we *allow* the seed that Source has planted within us to take root and bear fruit, we experience growth and fulfillment.

The four elements of nature we as Divine Feminine beings work with are *Sun, Moon, Water* and *Earth*. Each element represents an aspect of ourselves.

- The *Sun* element represents our sovereign conscious Self.
- The *Moon* element represents our subconscious Self. This is usually hidden from ourselves and shows up as our Shadow.
- The *Water* element is the most powerful element for use as a female. It represents our Feminine energy of flow and surrender.
- The *Earth* element represents our purpose, which is linked to our internal seed which grows when we come into a state of alignment and allowance.

You can use this visual grid to get a deeper understanding of yourself as a woman and how you can live a life of purpose, meaning, wholeness and vitality.

The Shadow to Self-Love program is a journey out of your Shadows and into one of love. This program helps you to uncover, transmute and heal your deepest Shadow wounds that cause negative, repeating toxic cycles in your life. This enables you to finally break free to live a life of joy, impact, fulfillment and peace.

To learn more about the *Shadow to Self-Love* program, access the link below.

http://shadowtoselfloveacademy.teachable.com

Please apply if this resonates with you, as I'd love to work directly with you to help you in your personal growth. In my program, I will help you to uncover your Shadow wounds and begin the process of healing your inner childhood traumas. This will allow you to begin to have more positive relationships with yourself and others. It will also allow you to unleash the amazing gifts that lie repressed within you. Are you ready to take the leap? Are you ready to answer the call to the new YOU – powerful, unstoppable, happy, peaceful, vibrant and magnetic?

THE SPIRIT OF A GODDESS

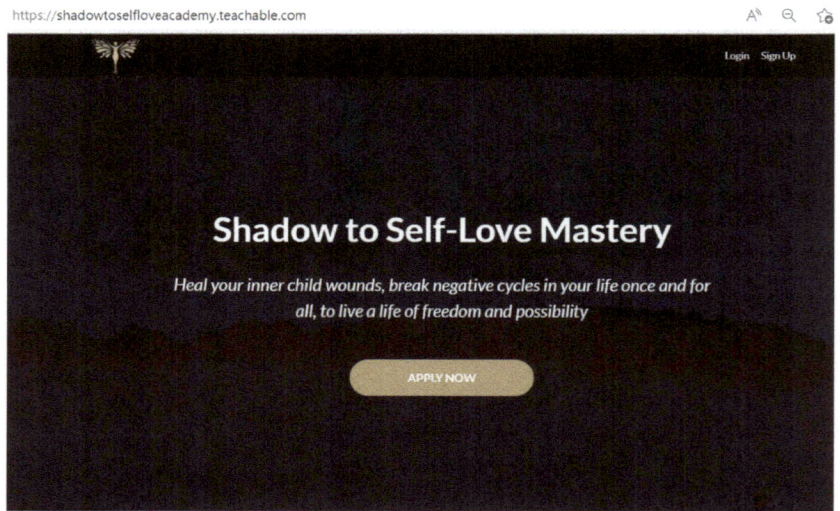

Are you struggling to break free of toxic relationships and/or negative repeating cycles in your life, once and for all?

Apply for my program above, and let's work together on the new, upgraded version of you!

14

Eternal Life

We are all Spiritual beings having a physical experience on earth. You are a Spirit incarnated in your physical form, living on this earth for a temporary amount of time. It's so easy for us to forget this because we spend what feels like forever living our lives, getting degrees, getting married, having babies, raising families, and so on. Then someone close to us dies, and it hits us hard and gives us a reality check. It reminds us that life is, indeed, temporary, and we need to cherish each day we have on this earth with each other as a gift.

Death is a subject a lot of us tend to avoid because it can be uncomfortable to discuss. One reason is fear of the unknown. Another is the confrontation of our mortality as a human being. We fear the pain associated with the death or loss of a loved one. In the Spiritual sense, however, there is really no death, but a transition to another realm of existence. Life is eternal, therefore, your Spirit lives on forever.

Death can be likened to a passenger getting on board a ship. The ship was never meant to be your permanent residence. When the ship reaches its final destination, you have no choice but to alight from the ship. You get distraught because you got too comfortable, started to have a party, and really began to believe that the ship was your home. Is it not so? You forgot the real purpose of the ship was to take you from point A to B. The transition from death of the physical Body back to your eternal Spiritual form is likened to alighting from this proverbial ship and continuing on our journey but in a different vehicle—your eternal Spirit.

There have been a lot of accounts of people who have had near-death experiences. Some have actually died and then woken up minutes after their heart stopped beating. Some died for a little longer, were officially pronounced dead by a medical professional and then woken up and described their experience in the Spiritual plane. I've read some of these accounts and compiled a list of similarities of their experiences. This is what I discovered.

WHAT HAPPENS WHEN YOU PHYSICALLY DIE?

- **You are immediately welcomed by your ancestors:** When you die, you are not alone. You are surrounded by your guardian angel and family members who have passed to meet you, comfort you and usher you into the Spiritual realms.

- **You are held accountable for your actions:** You are held accountable for the life you lived on earth. You are rewarded for the good and held accountable any words or actions wherein you knowingly caused others hurt or pain.

- **You have a glorified Spiritual Body:** Normally, this appears as a healthier, younger version of yourself, especially if you were very sick or had aged before passing. If you lived a good life and are welcomed into the kingdom of Heaven, your Spiritual Body emanates a bright, blinding white light that makes your skin appear to glow as if light rays are radiating from the pores of your skin.

- **You have a heavenly home:** You have a beautiful heavenly home where you will dwell forever.

- **Beautiful surroundings:** There are heavenly gardens, streams and rivers of living water that glisten and are healing

- **You have wings:** If you are given the role of an Angel, you have Angel wings and will be able to fly to different locations and move about at will.

- **You are omnipresent:** You have the gift of omnipresence—which is being at multiple places at the same time. You are not limited by space and time.

- **Your Divine assignments:** You are given Divine assignments to help other people on earth overcome their struggles, providing guidance, comfort and wisdom to bring them closer to Source.

With this in Mind, the end of life is something to be accepted and even embraced because if you live a good life, it leads to something magical and beautiful to behold in the Spiritual realm beyond your wildest dreams. Our goal is to keep our hearts pure, make use of our gifts and talents by fulfilling our purpose on earth and live a positive and meaningful life that can inspire others.

15

The Goddess Manifest

I've created the below Goddess Manifest for you to use as your daily Code of Conduct as a Goddess. To be called a Goddess, you must strive to meet the following tenets daily.

THE GODDESS MANIFEST

- I shall move with grace, ease and poise.
- I shall be kind to all.
- I shall not judge anyone, lest I be judged.
- I shall be slow to anger and quick to compassion and forgiveness.

- I shall only eat foods that nourish my Mind, Body and Spirit.
- I shall watch my words and only speak words of life, kindness, compassion, healing, love, blessings, upliftment and peace to myself and others.
- I shall watch my actions and ensure that my intentions are pure and forthright.
- I shall watch my thoughts and ensure that my thoughts are a high vibration of love and gratitude, knowing that my thoughts create my reality.
- I shall be mindful of what I listen to, read and watch, ensuring it is pure and of high vibration and knowing that my senses are a portal to my Spirit.
- I shall fully embrace, uplift and infuse love into my brothers and sisters.
- I shall be true to myself and show up authentically.
- I shall carry myself with grace and dignity with my head held high in honor of my ancestors, on whose shoulders I stand upon.
- I shall surrender fully to the ebbs and flows of life, trusting that all is in Divine order.
- I shall not force, fight, manipulate or chase anyone or anything but instead attract all that is meant for me.
- I shall maintain a peaceful disposition and surrender to the Universe and Source.

- I shall respect my Body as a temple and, therefore, treat it as sacred.

- I shall adorn my Temple Body so that my beauty on the inside is also reflected on the outside.

- I shall seek and follow my Earthly and Spiritual purpose and work to bring it to fulfillment.

When times get tough, I shall not run from challenges, but I will face them head-on with courage, integrity, dignity and self-respect.

I fully commit to being joyful and happy every day of my life.

When you are feeling down, say the following mantras to lift yourself up so you can step into the glory of the magnificent Goddess that you are.

The Spirit of a Goddess mantras

I am a magnetic Goddess of high vibrational frequency and I, therefore, attract all that is meant for me in Divine timing.

- I am an important and vital part of creation.

- I have a specific Divine purpose to fulfill on this earth.

- I am made in the Divine's image and likeness, and therefore, I shall walk this planet as a Goddess with grace, dignity, integrity, kindness, compassion and love.

- I have every right to be here on this planet.

- I welcome change with joy and acceptance.
- I give and receive love fully and abundantly

You are the Goddess. Let your light shine bright!

REFERENCES

AURA

https://www.consciouslifestylemag.com/human-energy-field-aura/ https://foreverconscious.com/7-layers-aura

INTUITION

https://www.livescience.com/54825-scientists-measure-intuition.html

Merriam Webster — definition of intuition Wikipedia — definition of intuition

https://www.dosomething.org/us/facts/11-facts-about-body-image (Girls Body image)

How to be a Magnetic Goddess: Embodying the Goddess — A Return to Sensuousness and Embodied Love — The Embodiment of Sensuousness—https://goddess-temple-of-love.mykajabi.com

https://goop.com/wellness/spirituality/healing-your-aura/ (Aura)

https://goop.com/wellness/spirituality/faith-in-the-times-of-covid-19/ (Faith in the COVID era)

http://www.thepsychicworkbook.co.uk/open-expand-aura/?doingwpcron=1589819050.49587988853454589843 7 5 (Expanding your Aura)

https://www.forbes.com/sites/brucekasanoff/2017/02/21/intuition-is-the-highest-form-of- intelligence/#2d9445f03860—Intuition

https://www.psychologicalscience.org/news/minds-business/intuition-its-more-than-a-feeling.html Intuition as a measurable by evidence

CLAIRVOYANCE

https://blog.sivanaspirit.com/sp-gn-intuitive-senses-strongest/

Empath: A Complete Guide for Developing Your Gift and Finding Your Sense of Self by Judy Dyer

ANGELS

9 choirs of Angels: https://catholicexchange.com/what-are-the-nine-choirs-of-angels

https://catholicism.org/more-qs-and-as-on-the-angels.html Angels & Time and Space

http://www.numerologist.com Lunar phases

www.ingramcontent.com/pod-product-compliance
Lightning Source LLC
Chambersburg PA
CBHW040733220426
43209CB00097B/1987/J